T0157177

Mary's Master

Colonization and the Indians in 17th Century New England

Leonard P. Judge

iUniverse, Inc.
New YorkBloomington

iUniverse books may be ordered through booksellers or by contacting:

iUniverse
1663 Liberty Drive
Bloomington, IN 47403
www.iuniverse.com
1-800-Authors (1-800-288-4677)

Because of the dynamic nature of the Internet, any Web addresses or links contained in this book may have changed since publication and may no longer be valid. The views expressed in this work are solely those of the author and do not necessarily reflect the views of the publisher, and the publisher hereby disclaims any responsibility for them.

ISBN: 978-1-4401-8817-6 (sc)
ISBN: 978-1-4401-8819-0 (dj)
ISBN: 978-1-4401-8818-3 (ebook)

Printed in the United States of America

iUniverse rev. date: 3/10/2010

Dedication

This work is dedicated to my wife Dorothy, who tolerated my accumulation of papers, books etc. spread about the house and those spread about the years involved in producing this work.

Also it is dedicated to my late sister Jean, who urged me to at least complete a shorter work when an eye problem interfered with the need to thoroughly review so many important or possibly important works needed to produce a work of greater detail and scope. Unfortunately she passed on just after reviewing the earliest part of "Mary's Master".

Thanks also to Sharon Hamlen who corrected my spelling, grammar and word usage.

Wickapimset- in the land of the Wampanoag

2009

Table of Contents

Tribal Domains and Significant Locations

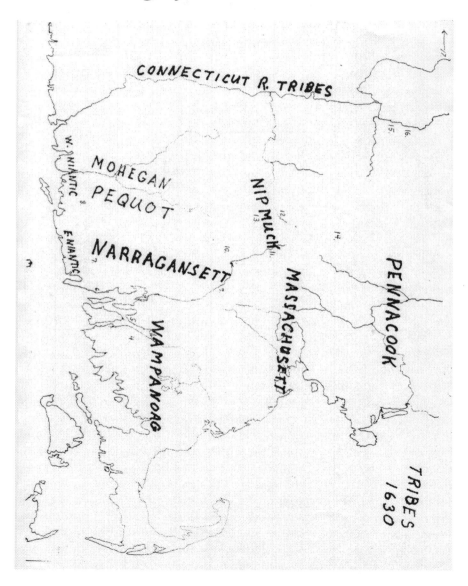

DOMAINS OF TRIBES OF SOUTHEASTERN NEW ENGLAND CIR. 1630

Plus Native Locations Significant in this History

1. Wessaqusett
2. Patuxet
3. Assawompset
4. Pocasset Swamp
5. Montaup
6. Pettaquamscut
7. Great Swamp
8. Mystic Fort
9. Pawtucket
10. Nipsachuck
11. Hassanemeset
12. Menameset
13. Quabaug
14. Wachusett
15. Squaheag
16. Pisgah
17. Schaghticoke

PREFACE

This is a historical account of the activities of the English colonists in southern New England through 1676 and their dispossession of the native's domains. Of natives, whose ancestors had lived in those lands for times unknown. (Perhaps the ancestors of the natives living in colonial times had in previous centuries displaced unrelated natives; we do not known nor does it seem those natives knew.) Research has continually pushed back the time that it is believed humans lived in the area. Occupation there, however, of more than twelve thousand years does not yet appear evident.

This account relates that colonization by English occurred not only in southern New England but in much of the present United States coastal area, bits of the southern hemisphere and many of the islands of the New World. Colonization by England had begun earlier in Ireland. References are made also to the other European states that were competitors with England for the new-found treasure of the western hemisphere.

This account focuses on the story of the colonization of New England, arguably, at least one of the most significant sub-stories of that long period. New Plymouth has been selected by historians as the archetypical colony to present as an honorable example of our country's founding. Massachusetts Bay colony (herein the colony will be called Mass.Bay to distinguish it from the tribe well known as the Massachusetts) has been honored as the primary resister to England's domination of the colonies. Rhode Island is honored as the colony introducing freedom of religion. If that history had been different- if the New England natives had completely defeated the New England English in the decade of the 1670's- we would not now have those three admirable stories in our national traditions. More significantly, then, all of the other natives of the east coast would have had an example of the vincibility of the English, a vincibility that to that time had never been shown but had always existed. The deterrent to future would-be colonists would have been extreme. These three colonies plus Connecticut were involved in King Philip's War of 1675-6 against some of the natives. This account states how the natives were at one point winning and how their effort rather suddenly collapsed. The account of the war includes excerpts from the famous narrative of one captive of that war, Mary Rowlandson. No other individual relates as much of intimate relations with the natives during that decisive war than she. Other English captives in later years inform us of more of the behavior of the natives in their stories. Tales of captives, such as Mary Jamison, Elizabeth Hanson, John Williams, John Gyles, Francis Slocum and many others are touched on herein. This story begins with Mary Rowlandson's capture. English captives may either meet with atrocious cruelties or kindness, respect and total acceptance. Indian captives in New England were almost always used in some form of servitude including slavery for the rest of their lives.

Rowlandson's relationship with her "master", Quanopin, a Narragansett sachem, while brief, is exceptional in that she expresses an admiration of him not expressed towards any other Indian. A similar admiration of Indian life and behavior by other captives in other times is also shown.

Generally this work questions the low esteem of Indian society imposed upon it both by early histories and modernism.

There are various spellings of individual Indians' names throughout by different sources and it can be suspected that such spellings were the best the English hearer could apply for the Algonquin name he heard. The particular spellings that appear in this work are my own arbitrary choices from other authors and may or may not come closest to the phonetic sound heard as those Indians spoke those names. If the reader reads from other sources, especially primary sources, he or she will surely see different spellings of what may appear to be the name of the same individual this also as well as with other nouns. Different spellings have caused difficulties to researchers in identifying individual Indians. Another problem was caused by Indians changing their name one or more times during their lives. I have tried to not misidentify any of the Indians, but it is still a possibility.

Language experts who have studied Indian languages have found basic similarities in certain Indian languages and have distinguished what they call language families, such as the Algonquian. Most of the tribes of the east coast of the present United States, including most of those mentioned herein, spoke an Algonquian language. The Mohawks dwellers of central New York, would be an exception as well as the Susquehannahock of Pennsylvania also mentioned who both spoke from a very different language family, the Iroquoian. The name Algonquian is derived from Algonquin, the name of a tribe living near the Ottawa River in Canada. There might be many different words in the speech of the Algonquins, proper, of Canada and the Wampanoag of Cape Cod, Massachusetts but their languages are both considered Algonquian. The Wampanoag and their neighbors the Massachusetts had little or no difficulty conversing with each other.

The word "tribe" is used generally to define the bonds of a society, and is applied to a people that are thought to have a common ancestor. I have chosen, in most instances, to call each village a tribe.

However, members of these villages in some cases recognize that they are related to the people of other villages and have a common name/identity for themselves and those of related villages- such names as Wampanoag and Narragansett. The villages of Pocasset and Mashpee, located forty miles apart, knew themselves both to be Wampanoag. The villages of Cowesett and Shawomet knew themselves to be Narragansett. Therefore it maybe appropriate to call the Narragansett, the Wampanoag, the Pequot, the Massachusett, the Nipmuck, tribes. However within southern New England (and probably other regions) many villages don't seem to have a family, a people, to whom they claim to belong , such as the Mohegan, the Connecticut River villages and villages in western Connecticut. Each of those are often called tribes. I have tried to make some clarity by often using compound names for villages of a common people, such as: Shawomet/Narragansett; Pocasset/Wampanoag; Mystic/Pequot.

Unfortunately if any of the contemporary English investigated Indian peoples' relationships, little of their thoughts on that subject got into writings before the severe disruption of the Indian world. The English design was only to divide Indians from each other when they felt a need to do so and only then were relationships considered of significance.

Quotes from contemporary sources are plentiful and identified, my own observations are easily discernible from other unidentified information sources.

In this work there are numerous extracts from authors denoted by pairs of quotation marks, ("- ") and also often quotes within quotes denoted by single quotation marks ('-') .

Within a quote the standard curved parenthesis symbol () is used to show the enclosed words are those of the author of the quoted section. The square cornered parenthesis symbol [ ] indicate enclosed words of an editor or myself within another's quote.

Leonard Judge

Chapter One

✦

Mary Rowlandson and Her Captors

On Feb.10th, 1676, old style calendar, the English town of Lancaster was attacked at the break of dawn by a body of Nipmuck and Narragansett fighters. This town was well fortified, as were most English towns, by buildings built extra strong called garrisons, whereto the English in other homes could flee in an attack. Lancaster had six garrisons. Lancaster was then on the fringe of Massachusetts Bay colony about 45 miles west northwest of Boston.

(England had not yet adopted the new calendar until 1752 when the date was advanced ten days and the first of the year made January 1 instead of March 21ˢᵗ as it was in the old calendar.)

Lancaster was settled in 1643 in territory occupied, time out of mind, by natives called Nipmuck. This attack was one of dozens that occurred in the conflict later called King Philip' War. The attackers set about burning the non garrisoned buildings and killing or taking captive English caught outside. With difficulty they, after two hours, set one of the garrisons ablaze. Within that garrison were 37 or more including Mary Rowlandson and her three children. It is Mary's narrative '' penned by the gentlewoman her self''', according to the anonymous writer of this narrative's Preface that gives us some insight into the character of the natives. {Rowlandson passim}

Mary White Rowlandson was born about 1637 in England of John and Joan White who came to Mass. Bay Colony and settled in Lancaster. {1Green p.24} They were said to be the largest landowners there. {2 Drake J.p123}

Mary married Rev. Joseph Rowlandson, probably in 1656 based on the date of their first child's birth in Lancaster records which was

Jan. 11 1658. That child named Mary, died on Jan. 20, 1661. They had three more children: Joseph, born Mar. 7, 1661/2; a second Mary born Aug. 12, 1665; and Sarah born Sept. 15,1669. Mary's (Sr.) age of death had always been assumed to have been about 41 because the name Mary Rowlandson disappeared from any records with only a few allusions that might indicate her living beyond 1678. However, a great research paper produced by David L. Green found that Mary remarried just nine months after the Reverend Joseph died, as recorded, on Nov. 24, 1678, at the age of 47. The Rev. and his family had moved to Wethersfield, Conn., in Apr. 1677. It was there Mary married the widower Capt. Samuel Talcott, father of eight, on Aug. 6, 1679. Mary Rowlandson became Mary Talcott on that day and thus disappeared to historians. {3Green p.31}

"According to the Wethersfield Vital Records, Mary Talcott, widow [Samuel died Nov.11, 1691] died on Jan.5,1710/11, age of about 73, having outlived the death usually given her by nearly 33 years." [4Green p.31}

The attack at that time was reportedly led by two Nipmuck sachems, Monoco (called by the English One-Eyed John) and Uskutugun (called Sagamore Sam), so we know Nipmunks were there. Mary says she was taken captive by a Narragansett as the English fled the burning garrison, so some of the attackers were Narragansetts.

The protagonist of the whole war was the Wampanoag sachem Pometacomet (called by the English Philip, and later King Philip). Early English writers called the sachem of the Pocanoket village of Montaup/ Sowams, the "Supreme Wampanoag Sachem." The designation supreme here is an English concept. Just how much power, authority, persuasion etc. any such sachem had with other Wampanoag villages is still not known.

Philip (we will use the better known name) was at the time located somewhere near Albany N.Y., usually thought to be at a Mahican village called Schagticoke. He apparently was trying to get other tribes to help him against the English. He may not have been aware of what was happening back to the east.

One thing that occurred while Philip was near Albany was that the Narragansetts, who had stayed out of any known involvement in the conflict going on between Philip and his allies and the Puritan Colonies, had been preemptively attacked by those Puritan colonies. The Colonies of Mass. Bay, Connecticut, and Plymouth were dominated by the religious sect called by their detractors, Puritans, a name the sect members themselves disliked. Those colonies had formed a defensive/offensive pact they called the United Colonies shortly after the Pequot War of 1637.

The Narragansetts had, since the conquest of the Pequot Tribe, been considered by the English as the most powerful tribe in New England that they would have to deal with. This and several other reasons seemed to have made the leaders of the Puritan colonies antagonistic toward the Narragansetts. Firstly, the Narragansett homeland or territory was almost the same land on which the non-Puritan colony of Providence Plantations and Rhode Island had planted, a place fled to by many English who rejected Puritanism or were rejected by the same. This made Rhode Island almost an enemy to its three neighbors, which also made it harder for the Puritan colonies to manipulate the Narragansetts. Secondly, the Mohegan tribe led by sachem Uncas became close allies or indeed lackeys of Connecticut and disputes between the Narragansetts and the Mohegans put Connecticut and the Narragansetts at odds. Thirdly, Plymouth feared Rhode Island was limiting it's own expansion to the west and making the Narragansetts part of that perceived problem. Fourthly, Conn. and Mass. Bay felt they should possess some of the land in the southern part of present Rhode Island. Attempts to gain such land went on until the Crown halted the disputes, at least temporarily, with the seemingly noble ruling that colonies could not gain land by war, in this case King Philip's War. Fifthly, in 1644 Samuel Gorton and Randall Holden dwellers of the Warwick area of Rhode Island and enemies of Mass. Bay convinced the Narragansett sachems that they could get the protection of the King if they produced and presented a letter of submission to the King. The letter was produced and accepted by the King. Mass. Bay then had to lay back in its' oppression of the tribe; however, Mass. Bay's anger was probably heightened by that. Fortunately for Mass. Bay, King Charles was in a civil war where the opposition was gaining and would in time defeat the royalty. Charles was defeated and in that war and beheaded in 1649. While he was so occupied in 1645, the United Colonies declared war on the Narragansetts, mobilized an army and sent for the sachems to parley. The sachems submitted to a so-called "treaty" requiring them to pay to the U.C. 2000 fathoms of good white wampum plus a tribute in wampum for each Pequot captive living with them. Payment of the tribute was often a problem for the Narragansetts. Also they were required to give up whatever former Pequot country they had been using since the Pequot war with such land going to the United Colonies.

This was but one of many extortions pressed upon the natives, some to be mentioned later. The English had acted aggressively against the natives several times, in the short time they had been in New England. In the development of the Pequot conflict, of 1636 the Pequots essentially had reacted to English aggression. The first fatal hostility of that war occurred when an Indian of the Massachusetts tribe, guiding a coercive English army through Pequot country, shot and presumably killed a Pequot. The reason for the incursion into that place goes back to the murder of one Captain Stone two years before the war. He was a free-lance trader from the West Indies, (an apparent scoundrel, threatened by both Mass. Bay and Plymouth with execution) who was killed, probably by Indians, when he sailed up the Connecticut river for trade. The Pequots were assumed to be the killers. Captain John Mason, however, leader of the attack on the Pequot fort at Mystic, wrote years later that the murdering Indians were not Pequots, and he should know as well as anyone. Mason in his history of the Pequot War, written some thirty years after that war, notes "these Indians [who supposedly killed Stone] were not native Pequots, but had frequent recourse to them, to whom they tendered some of those goods..." goods stolen from Stone's barque. Further he states, Stone "sailing into the Conn. River about 2 leagues [about 6 miles] from the Entrance cast Anchor...[he] procured some of those...Indians belonging to that place...to go as Pilots..."{5 Mason p.16} these he indicated were the killers. Even at that we can't know the circumstances of Stone's death; his own behavior might have gotten him into trouble with any Indian. Six miles up the river was territory of one of the so-called Connecticut

River tribes and not the Pequots, although some of the Pequots might have also been there at the time.

Another killing was that of one John Oldham, done off the coast of Block Island in July 1636. This was attributed, by the English, to the Block Island Indians, and the island was attacked by Mass. Bay for that reason. {6 Jennings p.206} The Commander of that attack says, conveniently, those Indians fled to the Pequots. That is very unlikely, since it would be a row of 33 miles over rough water to the closest known Pequot village at Mystic. The row to the southern shore of Rhode Island is about 13 miles, still difficult, and how many trips by a limited number of canoes would be needed to take all the natives from the island? That the natives hid-out somewhere on the island seems far more likely, just as the Commander said they had done the very day before. However, the English choose to blame the Pequots for both deaths, which helped to justify the attack upon them.

There is no evidence of any serious plan by any Indian group against the English (who were spreading everywhere) from 1620 until 1674 or 1675 when Philip did indeed seem to plot.

Chapter Two

◆

The War Begins

It was June 20th, 1675 when some of Philip's tribe began pilfering from abandoned homes in the town of Swansea, abandoned because of alarm over the continuing stories of Indian troubles. At one house with English still there, an Indian pilferer was shot and killed. This seems to have occurred on June 24th. As quickly as June 26 Mass. Bay sent Capt. Henchman with foot soldiers, Capt. Prentice with troops and Capt. Mosely with buccaneers to Swansea. Plymouth had sent soldiers even sooner than that.

On July 4, Capt. Hutchinson came from Boston to the headquarters of the assembled army at Swansea or Rehoboth with orders to depart from there with a force and to proceed to the Narragansett country. Official historian Hubbard wrote- "The next Morning was spent in Consultation how to carry on the Treaty...[they]...to make a Peace with a Sword in their Hands...all the Massachusetts Forces [went] over into the Narragansett country, to fight them, if...be need... as they passed, they found the Indians in Pomham's Country [Warwick R.I. area, the Shawomet/Narragansett village] all fled...".{7 Hubbard p.74} The army did venture further south in the direction of the supreme sachem's village, but for some reason, did not actually reach that village. At Pettaquamscott (about 15 miles south of present Warwick R.I.) they managed to get the names of four Indians onto the treaty composed by the English. Hubbard claims they were "Councellors and Attornies to Canonicus", the supreme sachem. Only one name, Corman, is a recognizable one, and he was associated with Ninigret, the Niantic/Narragansett sachem. The treaty was dated "July 15, 1675 Pettaquamscot" {ibid}

Although Mass.Bay had not sent forces to Swansea until June 26th, Plymouth may have sent a force there even before "mischief" by Pokanoket/Wampanoag occurred in Swansea. The deputy governor of Rhode Island John Easton in his "...Relacion..." noted that after a conference between six Rhode Islanders including Sam Gordon and himself with a group of Wampanoags including Philip, that he received a letter in Rhode Island from Plymouth "...sudingly..." after that conference. The conference was held "about a wecke before..." the outbreak of hostilities. That letter informed R.I. that they, Plymouth "intended in arems to Conforem philip...and in a weckes time after we had bine with the Indians the war thus begun. Plymouth soldiers were Cum to have ther head quarters within 10 mile of philip then most of the English there about left ther houses...in this time sum indians fell a pilfering sum houses that the English had left...". {8 Easton p.11} If Easton is correct Plymouth would seem to have had soldiers at Swansea before the pilfering of the Swansea homes, whereas most accounts indicate Plymouth only sent soldiers after Indian provocations.

A very telling letter Philip had had written for him in reply to one John Borden "a friend of Philip..." found in the Foster papers, gives a version of Philip's position on the interactions between the English and himself cir. 1675. In part it says - "At length a line of division was agreed upon between the English and my people, [specifically, he may be referring to a line set up by Plymouth in what the English called Swansea that was to preserve some Pokanoket land from English expansion] and I myself was to be responsible. Sometimes the cattle of the English would come into the fields of my people, for they did not make fences like the English.[Philip seems to have omitted what the Indians did to those cattle.] I must then be seized and confined till I sold another tract of my country for satisfaction of all damages and costs. Thus tract after tract is gone. But a small part of the dominion of my ancestors remains. I am determined not to live till I have no country".

While several skirmishes went on between Wampanoag and Plymouth forces at Rehoboth, Pocasset and Dartmouth, those of Mass. Bay and Connecticut were directed to bring the Narragansetts to submission and cooperation and their forces were sent into the Narragansett country. This led to the so- called treaty previously mentioned which was drawn up at the place called Pettaquamscutt (south of present day Saunderstown R.I.). No known sachem was there present. It was a demeaning set of demands, that is the wording was, but what was presented and how it was understood by the four Narragansetts contacted there could have been different. By the treaty terms, they were to seek out and kill any of Philip's subjects, male or female, that might enter Narragansett country and bring the slain to the English. They were to use the utmost of their ability in acts of hostility against their neighbors the Wampanoag. They were promised one coat for every dead Wampanoag brought in, but two coats for every live Wampanoag. Live Wampanoags could be sold into slavery.

Plymouth would soon sell " eight score" (160) Indians who had agreed to surrender at Dartmouth on about July 16-20,1675 on terms of some sort of security from the fray, terms that were overturned by authority at Plymouth.{10 Church p.50} Selling of captives was a diabolical way of getting rid of Indians who might be troublesome, eliminating the need to maintain the captives and gaining financially.

In noting previous English methods used in Ireland historian Slotkins sees a repetition in New England – Cromwell's "wholesale slaughter of the Irish and of his selling of many into West Indian slavery parallels exactly the policy adopted by the American Puritans in King Philip's War two decades later."{10b Slotkins p. 42}

After taking four Narragansetts, hostage to supposedly insure compliance with the treaty, the English force hurriedly left the area without ever meeting any of the well known Narragansett sachems.

The Mass. Bay forces then needed to get back to the opposite side of Narragansett Bay where the Wampanoag were assaulting several towns. The Conn. force was recalled to Connecticut because of a threat posed by Gov. Sir Edmond Andros of New York. Andros had sailed from New York, with troops on July 7, arriving at Old Saybrook fort located at the mouth of the Conn. River, in an attempt to assert authority over western Connecticut, long claimed by Andros' boss, James, the Duke of York. The attempt was disguised as protection for the people of that area from the Indians by New York but Connecticut leaders were almost as clever as Andros and blocked his landing with their own troops. The frustrated Andros didn't dare land and eventually sailed back to New York {11 Jennings p.307}.

A treaty dictated by the English such as Pettaquamscot, whether understood or agreed to by the Indians or not always had value, to their purposes. The English could use such a treaty as a pretext for punitive action when it suited them to point out violations of its' requirements. There indeed was a violation of that treaty, and the United Colonies did take punitive action in Dec. 1675. The Narragansetts had allowed at least two Wampanoag tribes, the Pocassets and the Sakonnet, Philip's nearest neighboring villages, to take shelter within their territory, but that was probably an act of humanitarianism not uncommon among native Americans.

The Pocassets and the Sekonnets seem to have been reluctant to rise up against the English probably out of fear not friendliness, but Philip certainly needed them when he fled his village of Montaup on June 29th to the eastern side of Mount Hope Bay. The Pocassets and Sekonnets, who dwelt there, were, thereby, drawn into the conflict when the English pursued Philip there. All three villages later fled with Philip toward the Nipmuck country.

On their journey to the Nipmucks, they were spotted by some residents of Rehoboth. The main English army was still then guarding a swamp at Pocasset where they thought the three Wampanoag tribes still were. A force gathered from Rehoboth, Mt. Hope and Swansea set out in pursuit of those Wampanoag. They were soon joined by 30 English from Stonington, Conn., 30 Providence men and 40 or more Mohegans-in all about 125 men- far less than the force still at Pocasset. However these volunteers obtained a significant happening for the English cause, a defection from Philip.

By marching into the night the volunteers reached the edge of a field called Nipsachuck, 20 miles northwest of Rehoboth, where their scouts reported that the Wampanoag were just beyond. In the morning of Aug. 1, they surprised the encampment of the Pocassets killing several, causing them to flee to where an apparently larger number of Wampanoags stopped the English and Mohegans. After some skirmishing the whole body of Wampanoag effected a successful withdrawal.

One of the Wampanoag who was shot and captured gave information that Ashwashonk, the Sekonnet squaw sachem had gone to the Narragansetts when the war began.

Capt. Nathaniel Thomas, who had led the volunteers, continued following the Wampanoags and was soon joined by Capt. Henchman with his six files of English and sixteen Massachusett Indians. Thomas was informed by his scouts that the trail had split and that "Wittaman" (Weetamoe the squaw sachem of Pocasset) had turned south towards the Narragansetts while the other Wampanoags headed north to Squabaug a Nipmuck town. Henchman, now in command, failed to follow either trail, much to Thomas' displeasure. {12 Thomas pp.227-233}

The information about the Pocassets and the Sekonnets leaving Philip comes from that letter probably sent to Gov. Winslow of Plymouth by "N.T." (evidently Capt. Nathaniel Thomas) who gives a first person account of the Rehoboth to Nipmuck country pursuit of the Wampanoags. In it he clearly says his scouts and a Pocasset prisoner both say the Pocassets and the Sekonnets diverted to the Narragansett country. Winslow kept this letter, and it was not discovered until 1792 and not revealed until 1855. None of the contemporary writers mention it.

Attacks upon English towns throughout eastern Mass. Bay soon occurred, including Rowlandson's Lancaster on Aug. 22 where eight English were then killed. By late Aug. the Connecticut River tribes joined the insurgency striking the settlements on the river.

Chapter Three

✦

Puritan and Narragansett Relations

The Narragansetts and the Indians who stayed with them were able to stay out of the war for six months, but the English were still concerned about them. Rumors were spread that the Narragansetts were secretly involved and that they harbored some of Philip's braves.

After an Indian attack on one of the Connecticut River towns, some of the English there said that the withdrawing attackers headed for Narragansett when really all that could be observed was the attackers exiting into the woods after the attack, this some 80 trail miles from the nearest Narragansett village.

Gov. John Winthrop Jr. of Connecticut had been concerned that the pressure put upon the Narragansetts in July might be too threatening and drive them to Philip's side. He wrote to his officers at Pettaquamscot on July 12, 1675: " Please to consider it be not far better to take up with such ingagements of amity [with the Narragansetts] as can be attained freely and willingly...then [than] that... all our neighboring heathen should be made open, professed enemies...nor... to be too strict in inquiry about persons fled to them...(if fled is better then with Philip)...". Winthrop was one of the commissioners of the United Colonies, so such good sense must have been presented to that body at some point in time. But despite such wisdom, despite the directive of Charles II that stated that without the permission of Rhode Island as required by the Royal charter of 1663 that they could not invade, - where it is written:

"It shall be unlawful for the rest of the Collonies to invade or molest the native Indians...within the bounds and lymitts here after mentioned... without the consent of the of the Governor and

Company of our Collony of Rhode Island & Providence Plantations".
{13 Arnold p.402 Vol.2}. There is no indication that Rhode Island
granted permission for an invasion. Despite all that and the immorality
of attacking those who have not been shown to be involved in the war
the United Colonies prepared to invade the Narragansett country.

What was written on the subject were these lines from Maj.
Gookin's "...Sufferings..." (a work dated Dec. 18,1677)- "But as we
were certainly informed that Philip was so distressed and clogged at that
time [at Nipsachuck], his ammunition almost spent, also the Squaw
Sachem and her people drawn off from them to the Narragansetts..."
All the same information that appears in Thomas's letter.

Gookin could have obtained such information from any of the
volunteers but especially from the Massachusett Indian guides. Gookin
had more control of the Massachusett Praying Indians than anyone else.
If Gookin says "we were certainly informed..." the English leaders had
to realize that those Indians who left Philip at that time had decided
to leave the warring faction and avoid combat by going to the Indians
at peace, the Narragansetts. Clearly then this was known prior to their
attack on the Narragansetts.{14 Gookin "Sufferings..."p.446 see note
#235}.Gookin was elected Major General of the Mass. Bay military
at one time and in 1675 he was a director of affairs with the Praying
Indians {15 Gookin "Sufferings..."p.425}. The name "Praying Indians"
was applied to those Indians that had been preached to of Christianity,
taught some prayers and effectively bought to a degree of submission
to English control.

Attacks upon English towns, even by the Nipmucks, were
justifiable if for no other reason but that the English were gradually
squeezing them from lands they had used from times unknown. The
Narragansetts were even more eminently justified in attacking by the
long documented record of Puritan oppression, coercion, and extortion
long preceding the preemptive attack of Dec.1675.

A review of some of the offenses committed by the English in their
relations with the Narragansetts is necessary here.

In 1637 the Puritans, with the important help of the former
Puritan, Roger Williams, convinced some of the Narragansetts to join
in an attack on the Pequots. The Pequots had also sought the help
of the Narragansetts at that time, so William's intercession was very

significant if we consider that the Pequots thought they had a chance of gaining the help of the Narragansetts at that time. None of the Puritan writers gave Williams any credit for his apparent successful effort, except perhaps, John Winthrop Sr. an important Mass. Bay leader and often governor who regularly communicated with Williams for years and had asked Williams to intercede against the Pequots.

The Narragansetts did go with the English war party that made the surprise attack on the Pequot town of Mystic on May 26,1637. Also there were Mohegans, forever English allies. During the attack some Narragansetts expressed dismay at the brutality of the Puritan slaughter of so many Pequots at the "fortified" village. They were said to have said too many Pequots were being killed. Such an expression was probably displeasing to the English, and the lack of a vigorous support by the Narragansetts was also displeasing to the attack leader Capt. John Mason of Conn. The devastation of the attack on Mystic must have been disheartening and frightening to the other Pequot villages. That day, the largest Pequot village, Weinshauk, located on the Shetucket (now the Thames River) about 8 miles away, rushed warriors to Mystic and engaged the withdrawing Puritans and their allies but with apparently little effect. In the following weeks the Pequots tried either to flee or hide while the English mounted searches to kill or capture Pequots, apparently doing the same to some other neighboring tribes that were not Pequots. The English were unable to know members of the different tribes, and perhaps not caring. Four weeks after the Mystic slaughter, Connecticut and Mass. Bay soldiers on a search and destroy mission went as far west as present New Haven where they thought some Pequots were hiding amongst another people called Quinnipiacs whom the English assaulted and pursued into a swamp. When the Indians sent out the women and children, they were all taken captive to be used as servants, even though Mason acknowledges some were "Indians belonging to that Place..." {16 Mason p.40}. The captives taken in these round ups were divided among the English, Mohegans, and Narragansetts. These captive assignments were often sources of troubles between the three.

The avowed purpose of the break-up of the Pequots, per some English writers, was to remove the name of Pequot from the minds of men, and although that never was accomplished, a sort of a genocide was once an objective to some.

In 1643 Miantonomi, sachem of the Narragansett village located in present Kingstown R.I., and considered "supreme sachem" of the Narragansetts, attacked sachem Uncas' Mohegans. Perhaps this was to avenge the Mohegans earlier attacking some Narragansett hunters hunting in former Pequot territory or perhaps it was because Uncas had threatened a Connecticut river tribe allied to the Narragansetts. Miantonomi was captured at that time and brought by the Mohegans to the Connecticut capital at Hartford where the Commissioners of the United Colonies in their first assembly decided Miantonomi had violated the "Hartford" treaty of 1638. That treaty had said Indians had to get Connecticut's approval before attacking other Indians. Mass. Bay's treaty of 1636 said the Narragansetts must get its approval before attacking other tribes. Jennings writes: "Massachusetts had regarded that treaty [Connecticut's.] as null and void and had required Miantonomi to deal with Boston rather than Hartford. Since Miantonomi had in fact consulted John Winthrop, Sr., before attacking Uncas, in accordance with the only obligation that Massachusetts then recognized, and Winthrop had authorized the Indian ' to take his own course', the Commissioners...had on their hands a basket full of pretensions, claims and obligations that none of them wanted to sort out in public discussion." {17 Jennings p.267} Perhaps Winthrop was not involved with the Commissioners when they directed Uncas to take Miantonomi into his country and execute him there. Uncas complied. The Narragansetts claimed they had arranged and paid a ransom and were dismayed when they heard of the execution. The directive to the Mohegans to take Miantonomi to their country and there execute him was, I am sure, the often used strategy of reinforcing hostility between tribes for the benefit of the English. Roger Williams who claimed Miantonomi as his close friend was at that time in England so he could not intervene if indeed he would have.

It should be pointed out that these treaties were composed by Englishmen, written in English and with requirements and restrictions only on the Indians who obviously had no input. One observable exception was the request made at Pettaquamscot where one clause requested that there be no efforts permitted by missionaries in

Narragansett, which could have been the idea of an Indian or an English officer present there then who would not want to have a missionary meddling in the Narragansett country at that time.

One could and should ask who were these people with only ten to forty years on this side of the ocean making rules through the writing of treaties that the native people were to agree to and follow.

It is questionable how much the natives understood of the English treaties or why they would agree to them if they did understand. From the English side, coercion was certainly used, and there was always the aforementioned prospect of using any semblance of a violation to threaten punitive action or to make more demands. From the Indian side with whatever understanding they had of the danger to their interests, they might seem to comply but really only temporized, causing future problems.

In 1660 the United Colonies charged the Narragansetts with a number of crimes and imposed a fine of 595 strands of wampum. Wampum in those years was the medium of coin used in New England. The Indians knew they would have difficulty paying this in the allotted time. One Humphrey Atherton of the Atherton Co. came forward with a mortgage scheme that paid the fine and then somehow tried to foreclose on that mortgage whereby the company could claim ownership of a large piece of land (most of south-central R.I.) However the now chartered colony of Rhode Island was able to interfere with the claim by the power of their charter.

In 1664 the Crown sent four royal commissioners with the fleet sent to subdue the Dutch colony of New Amsterdam. After which the commissioners were to investigate the activities of the United Colonies, especially that of Mass. Bay. According to historian Fransis Jennings, "They discovered the fraud of the Atherton mortgage so incontrovertibly that John Winthrop Jr. (son of John Winthrop Sr. and a member of the Atherton Co.) did not even attempt to defend it."{18 Jennings p.285} It was at this time that the commissioners called the United Colonies "The usurped authority".

Conn. Gov. Winthrop Jr., Gov. Josiah Winslow of Plymouth, Richard Smith of Wickford R.I., George Denison, Mass. Bay Capt. Edward Hutchinson and Mass. Bay Commissioner HumphreyAtherton were all associated with the Atherton Co.

Chapter Four

✦

The Preemptive Plans

The next major interaction with the Narragansetts was the so-called treaty at Petaquamscot, which of course was considered as valid by the English; so when the Sekonnets and the Pocassets were accepted by the Narragansetts into their country, the treaty was violated, and the English threatened the Narragansetts.

The summer and fall of 1675 saw numerous attacks upon the English people and towns of Mass. Bay and Plymouth colonies, especially in the Connecticut River valley. The tribes of that valley had joined the Wampanoag and the Nipmuck against the English. The English now felt threatened in all but the eastern most towns.

The English military effort was mostly ineffective up to that time. One Indian village after another joined in this war begun by Philip, even many tribes northeastward along the coast of New Hampshire and Maine who had never probably never seen Philip became active. The English heretofore had been confident that they could manipulate these Indian people (even though contempt and distrust in all other matters was the general attitude toward them). Events now destroyed that confidence.

Now if most of the tribes had joined the battle, why wouldn't the Narragansetts whom the Puritans had treated so badly also turn on the English? Now here was a "good" reason to strike the Narragansetts preemptively. Indeed not only would it be a "good" reason, but probably it was one of the prime real reasons, however, not one to be readily admitted since it might indicate themselves as causing such hostility in the Narragansetts.

The United Colonies ordered the Narragansetts to turn over all the Wampanoag that might be with them by Oct. 28th 1675. Such an order might push the tribe into the war if indeed it was really conveyed thusly to the Narragansetts. Then again what was written that they said and what was actually said to the Narragansett sachems could easily be different.

The deadline passed, and it was written that the "supreme" sachem's (Canonchet) reply to it was "No not a Wampanoag nor the paring of a Wampanoag nail", an unbelievable response from someone who we are told reaffirmed the Pettasquanscot treaty on Oct. 18th. What is known for sure is that the United Colonies prepared to invade the Narragansett country. They must have known that this would bring the Narragansetts into the war, but perhaps they expected they would achieve a crushing defeat of the Narragansetts as they had against the Pequots forty years earlier.

In preparation for the invasion a day of "humiliation and fasting" was ordered for Dec. 2 1675. They might have fasted, but was there humiliation in New England ?

The U.C. Planned for a force of 1500 men. The Mass. Bay contingent set out from Boston on Dec. 8th. That colony had promised its soldiers land in addition to their pay. Most of the soldiers grew old and died before any of the promised land was given out. Had Mass. Bay anticipated giving out some of the conquered Narragansett land? The right to conquered land in the Narragansett country was nullified by the "Order of the Privy Council [essentially the Crown] Dec.13, 1678" two years after the conflict.

The Mass, Bay force crossed over the Patuxet River into the vicinity of the Narragansett villages of Shawomet, Cowesett, and Potowomut and marched through sachem Punham's Shawomet village on Dec. 12 .{19Hubbard p.139 } "They were no sooner arrived in the Narragansett country, but they took and killed above forty Indians." {20 I. Mather p. 107} Capt. Mosely's men captured or killed 36 Indians, one of which he took as a guide as far as the Narragansett fort in southern Rhode Island. {21 Hubbard p.134} Was this Peter, the Indian referred to by Deputy Gov. John Easton in his "Relation" where he wrote "...it is true the indians generally ar very barbarus peopell but in this war I have not herd of their tormenting ani but that the English army Cote an old indian and tormented him ..."? {22 Easton p.13} I. Mather has it that an Indian traitor approached the English and promised to lead them to the Indian fort at the main Indian gathering location{23 I. Mather p.107}

Capt. Mosely had under his command buccaneers hired by Mass. Bay. Part of the understanding between him and Mass. Bay was that these men "would not be bound up in ...marches or executions to particular places..." and would keep all the Indian goods and sell those Indians they captured as their own reward. {24 Jennings p.311}

"Dec.14 five files sent out under Sag. Bennet killed one man and one woman and brought in four more...the whole company after marched into the Sachem's country [Punham's, Shawomet] where they burnt 150 wigwams, killed 7...brought in 8..."- "The next Day ...Stone Wall John [an Indian known to the English] pretending to come from the Sachems, intimating their willingness to have Peace, yet [he] could hardly forebear threatening, vapouring of their numbers and Strength...-this treatherous Fellow, some of his Crew, as he went home, met some of Capt. Gardner's Men... and slew his sergent with one or two more. Two also of Capt. Oliver's Men..." {25 Hubbard p.140} Note that before Dec.15th the Narragansetts had not committed any hostilities while the English had killed or captured 57 Narragansetts and burnt 150 wigwams, this by their own accounts.

Whether there was sincerity in the peace offerings by the Indians, the intention of the English seems apparent enough. They intended to attack and destroy Narragansetts wherever they could find them. They assembled their army of 1400 to 1500 men, having added the Connecticut force, Mohegans and acontingent of Pequots under Capt. John Mason Jr.. This was the largest army assembled up until that time in the present U.S.. They advanced to the Narragansett fort (located in a swamp in present Kingstown R.I.) through the snow and attacked the fort on Dec.19, 1675. It was claimed that they were led by the captive Peter without whom it is also claimed that they would not have been able to find the fort, but that is unlikely since they had a large body of Mohegans with them who would be knowledgeable of the fort's location. There was probably enough intercourse between Mohegans and Niantics that knowledge of any "fort" established by the Narragansetts would have reached the Mohegans. It was Niantics that went to the site and buried the dead Indians.

The official and paid chronicler of the war, Rev. William Hubbard (paid 50 pounds, equal to $10,000 in 1965 money){26 Burke p.254}, in one of his justifications for the attack upon the Narragansetts, wrote that "besides the favoring of those that fled to them and supplying the whole Body of the [warring]Indians with Victuals upon all Occasions [and]... that in all the late Proceedings of the Enemy many of their young men were known to be actually in Arms against us; many of whom were found either wounded in their Wigwams or were occasionally seen returning after Exploits aboard, to be healed of their wounds at home." But earlier Hubbard writes "...without his [Peter's] Assistance our Men would have been at a Loss to have found the Enemy..." . {27Hubbard P.136} So we are to believe the English had seen Narragansetts, wounded, returning to their wigwams and yet the English could not locate the Narragansett fort!

These conflicting stories are likely examples of fabrication so easily created to serve English justifications. Fabrications are created to present untruths about the Indians who do not know what has been written or to refute what they may suspect has been written. Sometimes the English writings do contradict thereby indicating fabrication by one or both sources. Concerning the English attack on the Pequot fort at Mystic, the Rev. Philip Vincent wrote a narrative of the Pequot War in which, at one point, he relates that as the English approached an entrance to the fort- "The English went resolutely up to the door of the fort- 'What! Shall we enter?' said Capt. Underhill 'What come we for else?' answered one Hedge...who advancing before the rest, plucked away some brushes and entered. A stout Pequot encountered him, shoots his arrow...into his right arm, where it stuck. He slashed the savage...who pressing toward the door, was killed by the English...". {28 Vincent p.103} Underhill seeing Vincent's story must have been offended and wrote in his own later narrative- "Worthy reader, let me entreat you to have a more charitable opinion of me than is reported in the other book...Myself approaching to the entrance, found the work too heavy for me to draw out all those [tree branches] which were strongly forced in. We gave order to one Hedge and some other soldiers to pull out those brakes. Having done this...and without orders...proceeded first on the south side of the fort." Underhill next stated he had never said "shall we enter", or questioned anyone whether they should enter the fort as that was unfitting an officer.{29 Underhill p.25} But fabrications worked quite well down through the decades, and many modern histories seem to overlook contradictions as indicators of fabrications in other doubtful relations. Historian Cave sees contradiction there but tends to believe Vincent.

Chapter Five

✦

The Great Swamp Fight

The attack on the Narragansett fort, later called the "Great Swamp Fight", would seem to have been a success, with the English driving the Indians from the fort and setting the wigwams ablaze, even though they received considerable loss. One anonymous narrator, who seems to have been a participant, wrote "we" were driven back out of the fort after the first penetration "by an unexpected recruit of fresh Indians...". {30 "factor"/Drake I.C. p.362} Perhaps Narragansetts from other villages arrived to assist the regular occupants.

Mather wrote "...many men, women and children were burned in their Wigwams...it is supposed that not less than 1000 Indian Souls perished at that time." [31 I. Mather p.108}.That figure was a likely exaggeration; the noncombatant Indians probably had time and opportunity to escape the fort as the situation deteriorated.

Capt. Ben Church's son Thomas wrote the most extensive biography of any participant in the war. In that work Capt. Church tries to dissuade the commander of the army, Joshua Winslow, from his order to burn all the wigwams because Capt.Church felt the wigwams would be valuable to the English for shelter. He however makes no mention of those so often referred to, " valuable prisoners", nor do any of the other accounts, which may indicate that the noncombatants were able to escape if not killed beforehand. The number of Indians who died in the assault plus those who died later from wounds or exposure would be impossible to determine. Ninigret had sent some of his men to the swamp after the battle and made a report of 22 Indian "captains" dead left there but that was only those left behind. The loss to the English seemed to be over 80 plus whatever Mohegans were killed, with 100 to

150 wounded. {32 Hubbard p.155} The number of wounded English that survived were helped by treatment of them the next day in homes on Aquidneck Island. Occasionally, mention of the later deaths from wounds then suffered by English participants in the Swamp Fight is seen in various writings. The Puritans were thereby assisted by the somewhat neutral Rhode Islanders, but such assistance to wounded Wampanoag, if indeed that happened by neutral Narragansetts, was considered intolerable by the Puritans and was one of the stated grounds for the invasion of the Narragansetts.

A significant account in Church's narrative provides evidence indicating the Sekonnet tribe was dwelling with the Narragansetts at the time of the Swamp Fight. "Some time after this fort fight a certain Sekonnet Indian hearing, Mr. Church relate the manner of his being wounded, told him, [that] he did not know but he himself was the Indian that wounded him, for that he was one of the company of Indians that Mr. Church made a shot upon, when they were rising to make a shot [at the English]. They were in number about 60 or 70 that just then came down from Pumham's town and never before then fired a gun against the English"{33 Church p. 63}. That might indicates the number of Sekonnet warriors dwelling with Pumham and also that they were not involved in a earlier ambush of Church in present Tiverton R.I.. Capt. Church had begun conversations with the Sekonnets in July of 1676 when he found them back in their own lands following their second desertion from Philip.

All the Naragansett villages seem to have been deserted after the Swamp Fight except the Niantic village, its sachem Ninigret somehow managing to keep his village out of the conflict.

The Narragansetts wandering in the forests made a couple of attempts at peace. When would they ever learn who they were up against? Hubbard in another apparent fabrication tells the reader that two Narragansetts came to the English on Jan. 7 "to make way for a Treaty of Peace". He says they blamed Canonchet in that he had misinformed their tribe about the treaty terms. But the Reverend says that they lied, and it was so known because "by chance" some English found a copy of the [Pettaquamscutt] "Treaty" inside a wigwam abandoned in the attack of the fort . Really, some Indians were sitting in the wigwam reading the treaty and then ran off leaving the paper inside! How many Narragansetts could even read English? It is even difficult today for English readers to decipher the scribbling of those times. {34 Hubbard p. 157}

Hubbard writes "Jan. 10 Fresh Supplies of soldiers came up from Boston". Earlier supplies had been delivered to the army by boats, and the army did continue searching for and capturing Indians here and there. {35 Hubbard p.161}

Mather recounts the killing and or capture of about 70 Indians after the Dec.19 battle until the disbanding of the army on or about Feb.16th 1675/6. The English by that time were so short of food that they killed their own horses for food.{36 I.Mather .pp108-110}

Sometime in late Jan. or early Feb., some of the Narragansetts reached a Nipmuck encampment where, it was reported, the Nipmuck, apprehending them as enemy, did fire upon them. That mistake was discovered, and the Nipmuck joined forces with the Narragansetts and supposedly the Pocasset and Sakonnet /Wampanoag. Their first joint effort was the attack on Mary Rowlandson's town of Lancaster. The author of "a Factor", in his narrative writes that attack took place two days after the army's disbanding and probably his discharge.{37"factor"- Drake "Indian Captivities.."p.364}

Chapter Six

◆

Lancaster Attacked

Mary's description tells us the Indians attacked "about sun-rising". From one house five were taken "the Father, Mother and a suckling Child, they knockt [clubbed] on the head, the other two they... carried away...Another ...running along...shot ...fell down... begged for his life...[they] knockt him in the head and stript him naked and split open his bowels...".{Rowlandson passim}Those unfortunate individuals had failed to reach the nearest garrison.

Lancaster had been attacked back on Aug. 22nd of the previous year, so another attack should not have been a surprise. The night of Feb.9th most of Lancaster's residents had gathered into the five widely scattered garrisons. There were 14 soldiers and 50 men in the town. {38 Ellis & Morris} Mary's husband the Rev. Rowlandson was away at Boston seeking a greater military presence. The Rowlandson garrison was the only one breached.

The Indians had managed with difficulty to set the Rowlandson garrison ablaze as Mary says "with Flax and Hemp which they got out of the barn...I took my Children to go forth and leave the house". As she and others opened the door, shots poured upon the house, "but out they must go". One shot passed through Mary's side and the hand and bowels of her youngest child, Sarah, who Mary was then carrying. Mary's elder sister's son had his leg somehow broken and the Indians seeing this, they "knockt him on head", possibly only wanting able bodied captives. Mary's elder sister was hit by a bullet and died shortly after her son's murder.

"N.S."(who was likely Nathaniel Saltonstall a contemporary writer of 1675) wrote an account of the war in which he told of one of Mary's sisters being taken captive that Feb.10th and directed it to readers back in England - "...that you may perceive the malicious Hatred of these Infidels have to Religion and Piety ... As they were leading them ["... Rowlandson and two sisters of her own..."] away ... one of the Sisters being big with Child going into the Woods to be privately delivered, the Indians followed and in a jeering Manner, they would help her, and be her Midwifes and thereupon they ript up her Body, and burnt the Child before her Face, and then in a merciful Cruelty to put her out of Pain, knockt her o'th Head." {39 Saltonstall p.83}

Mary's narrative has nothing like this at all. She does say her eldest sister Elizabeth was shot dead in the doorway of the garrison. The editor of one edition of Mary's narrative, Charles Lincoln in a footnote lists only two sisters, Hannah Divoll the youngest and Elizabeth Kerley the eldest. {40 Lincoln p.119} In another contemporary account this appears- " On the 11th of May [1676] two of our captives were returned by Ransom...one of them the Sister of the Wife of Mr. Rowlandson... and another woman taken out of the same House."{41 "a True Account"p.258} The surviving sister would be Hannah Divoll.

Although "N.S.'s" third narrative or letter published in England covers from Mar. 1676 through July 1676 and he had then heard of Mary's treatment by her captors and wrote that they " in there rude Manner seemed to show her great respect..." {42 Saltonstall p.83}, he could not have then seen her narrative published in 1682 when he wrote in July 1676, or known of the later release of Hannah Divoll or probably even of the death of Elizabeth Kerley.

Certainly there were other stories of atrocities committed by the Indians but perhaps not as bad as this one, concerning Mary's sister, apparently maliciously created by N.S. before other accounts would indicate that it never happened. Decades later, Cotton Mather would tell other very similar stories of captives taken in later times. Were such stories of his modeled on "N.S.'s"?

The Indians began to draw off those who had come out of the garrison directing them to come with them. Mary asked if they would kill her? They answered she would not be hurt as long as she accepted captivity. From that garrison, twelve were killed, twenty-four taken captive and one adult and 3 children managed to escape.

Mary comments about the moment of capture: "I had often before this said, that if the Indians should come, I should chuse rather to be killed by them then [than] taken alive but when it came to the tryal my mind changed; their glittering weapons so daunted my spirit, that I chose rather to go along with those (as I may say) ravenous Beasts, then that moment to end my dayes;..."

"N.S." again has more to write about these terrible Indians in his "New and Further Narrative..."- "... many Colonists have been destroyed with exquisite Torments and most inhuman Barbarities; the Heathen rarely giving Quarter to those they take, but if they were Women, they first satisfie their filty Lusts and then murder them."{43Saltonstall p.98} Such was the widely held expectation of many or most English before there was any evidence of sexual abuse by New England Indians.

That night, the Indians, with their captives and booty of farm animals, withdrew to George's Hill, still within sight of Lancaster. There they slaughtered some or all of the animals "miserable was the wast that was there made [of those animals]... Oh the roaring, and singing and dancing, and yelling of those black creatures in the night, which made the place a living resemblance of hell".

That night they were near a deserted English dwelling. Mary asked if she could spend the night there, they answered, "what will you love English [person]...still?" Here we see she is making a rather large request of her captors, captors she had thought of as merciless beasts then and before her capture.

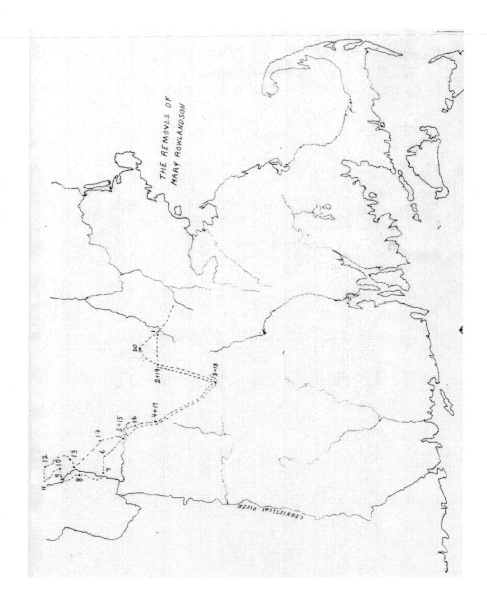

Key To Locations Of Removes During Mary Rowlandson's Captivity

1. Lancaster – George's Hill
2. Near to Mt. Wachusett, present Princeton Ma.
3. Menameset or Wenimesset Indian village on the Ware River
4. Nichewaug Indian village
5. north side of the Baquaug (Miller's River)
6. a swamp near English town of Northfield Ma.
7. Squaheag near Northfield
8. Coasset near present South Vernon, Vt.
9. Ashuelot Valley N.H.
10. Ashuelot Valley N.H.
11. near Mt. Pisgah N.H.
12. near Mt. Pisgah N.H.
13. near present Hinsdale N.H.
14. south of Northfield Ma.
15. North side of the Baquaug (Miller's River)
16. South of the Baquaug
17. Nichewaug
18. Menameset
19. Same as #2
20. Mt. Wachusett

Information of these locations mostly from Lincoln

Chapter Seven

✦

The Removes Begin

The following day the whole body, captives and captors moved on into the forest. "It is not my tongue, or pen can express the sorrows of my heart and bitterness of my spirit that I had at this departure; but God was with me."

One Indian took Mary's child upon a horse with him in an apparent consideration of the child's wounded and weak condition, but the child moaned so much crying, " I shall die, I shall die!", that Mary took her from the horse and carried the six year old child until Mary's strength gave out and she fell. Next, the Indian placed the two upon the horse, again showing some kindness. But as they descended a steep hill, Mary and child slid over the horse's head to the ground- "at which they like inhuman creatures laught and rejoyced to see it...But the Lord renewed my strenght and carried me along...". Just how the Lord carried her along Mary does not say, but my suspicion is that it was the horse that carried the two along. After the fall, she notes that snow began to fall, and when night fell they halted. She sat all night by a "small fire" in the snow with Sarah upon her lap. Scholars say that second night was located near to Mt. Wachusetts.

The next day Mary, Sarah and an Indian were all placed upon a horse, apparently to transport the wounded child and Mary without them falling off. Mary would credit God for the favor rather than the men who chose to do it and the poor horse that bore the three.

That afternoon, they reached the Indian town of Wenimesset which was "Norward of Quabaug"; the remove between these two guessed at locations would be about 18 miles, quite a hike on dry pavement and much harder through snowed-on woods. Mary was at this location Feb.

29

12th to Feb. 28th. "That day" [Feb.13] {44 Lincoln p.124} one Robert Pepper, an English soldier who had been captured in Sept. 1675 came to see Mary. He had heard of Mary's coming into that town and obtained leave to go to see her. Now that is remarkable, if an adult male captive is allowed to move about without close observation doesn't that suggest a very loose captivity? He told Mary he had been with his captors as far as Albany N.Y. to see Philip. Pepper had been wounded in battle when a body of English soldiers under Capt. Beers was almost totally destroyed by the Indians when they attempted to relieve Northfield on September 4th, 1675. He had been unable to walk and was carried by his captors until well enough to walk. At a later date, he managed to get away from his captors and made his own way home; he claimed he was not unkindly treated during his captivity.

While Mary's wound healed Sahara continued to fail and nine days after the wounding, "without any refreshment of one nature or other, except a little cold water" the child died, "Feb.18th". Mary said her child had moaned day and night all those days and some Indians had threatened her that her master would knock the child in the head if she did not stop moaning. The statement that the child went nine days without any refreshment of any kind is inconsistent with the parceling of food to captives by Indians in this and other first person accounts.

Mary laments that previously she "could not bear to be in the room where any dead person was, but now the case is changed; I must and could ly down by my dead Babe, side by side all the night after". God only, she says, preserved her from suicide then. The next day, with Mary still clinging to her dead child, some Indians told her she must go to see her "master" at another wigwam. When she tried to take the child with her, they insisted she must go alone. Mary did comply, but at the first opportunity she found, she went back to the first wigwam where she found that her daughter's body was gone. Mary asked the Indians there where the child was? They told her "upon the hill" and led Mary to a newly dug spot where they said they had buried the child. This would seem to have been a considerate way of handling this sorrowful death under the circumstances.

At this time Mary notes- "...by my Master in this writing, must be understood Quanopin who was a sagamore, and married King Philip's wive's Sister; not that he first took me, but was sold to him by another Narraganset Indian, who took me when I first came out of the Garison". "Master" was an English concept meaning he who possessed the services and most the time of the servant. Nothing quite like that existed in these New England native societies; certainly Quanapin was not Mary's "master". Mary notes that she was given some burden to carry when the party made their "removes" but so did all the Indians. She never mentions doing anything directly for him. Quanapin had given a gun to the Indian who first took Mary captive in exchange for her and that is how she became his captive.

After that, Mary had the liberty to go and see her ten year old daughter Mary, who was elsewhere in the same village. Mary, the mother, complained they had little opportunity to visit each other. When the daughter first saw Mary she began to cry, whereupon the Indians there told Mary she must leave. Mary went back to her own area, and while bemoaning her sad situation, her son Joseph came to her. He was being held by a "smaller parcel of Indians...at a place about six miles off". His master had gone off on an attack on Medfield (some 50 miles direct distant from that encampment) on Feb. 21, and the master's squaw had brought Joseph to visit Mary and before that to visit his sister. This Mary took as an "answer to earnest and unfeigned desire" having "entreated the Lord". There is no expressed appreciation of the Indian's apparent kindness.

One of the warriors returned from the attack on Medfield with plunder, which included a Bible which he offered to Mary. She gladly accepted it and asked if he thought the Indians would allow her to read it; he answered yes. Mary thanked "the wonderful mercy of God to me".

There were seven English children, goodwife (an English name applied to most wives) Joslin and Mary at that village. Mary knew the Indians intended to move on and that her party would take a different course than the Indians with the other captives, so Mary went to talk to Joslin. Joslin was to deliver a child within "but one week" and had also a two year old child with her there. Joslin confided to Mary that she hoped to escape; Mary urged her not to attempt it.

Mary later heard of the murder of Joslin "as some of the company told me in my travel". Joslin, Mary was told, apparently continually beseeched her captors to let her go home. "Vexed with her importunity" they took her, stripped her naked, placed her in the center of a circle, "knocked her on head and the child with her", then they made a fire and put the mother and child in it. The other English children were warned the same would happen to them if they attempted to escape or to complain. Clearly, if accurate this was an atrocity. Elizabeth Howe, 17, a resident of Marlborough was visiting her sister Ann (Howe) Joslin at Lancaster on the day it was attacked. Elizabeth was captured and later released. If Ann was "goodwife Joslin", she fared much worse than her sister.

Apparently at that time, Mary's party was fleeing an English army, probably Mass. Bay and Connecticut forces under Capt. Savage. The Indians sent some of their men back to hold off the English while the rest moved on to the Bacquaug River (now the Miller River.) Here they required two days to cross, doing so by building rafts on the spot. So the English army was delayed or sidetracked for two days. Mary notes that she stayed dry on the crossing while many Indians got soaked. Also she "was somewhat favored," in the amount of burden she was obliged to carry because of her wound.

Now Mary notes "The first week of my being among them I hardly ate anything; the 2nd week, I Found my stomach grow very faint for want of something, and yet it was very hard to get down their filthy trash but the 3rd week, though I could think how formerly my stomach would turn against this or that...yet [now] they were sweet and savoury to my taste." Mary's lack of food in the first week must have been due to her inability to eat Indian food, not that she wasn't offered something.

It was on Monday March 6th that the Indians picked up and left the village on the northwest side of the Baquaug where they had stayed, burning the wigwams as they left. Did they, thereby deny their use to the English, who couldn't figure out a way to cross the river anyway? It was Mary's 6th remove. She notes the English army arrived that day, and saw the smoking wigwams but were stopped by the river. Mary marveled at the way in which all of the Indians, "the greatest number [who] were Squaws..." managed to cross the river while the army would not attempt it.

Mary's interpretation of the various ways by which the Indians prevailed over difficulties (i.e. the river crossing) was that God assisted them at times, but only for a time, in order to chasten the English.

Mary was a very prejudiced person; probably the Puritan English were more so than the general English population. The English, in general, felt themselves superior to other societies - the French, the Spanish, the Dutch (which feeling was probably reciprocal by them) but especially to the "barbarians" which title included the "wild Irish", the Indians and the Africans. Added to this was the sense in the Puritans that God was primarily concerned with their relationship to Him while others did not enjoy that special concern.

Chapter Eight

✦

Mary Jamison

A comparison of Rowlandson's narrative with the captivity narrative of another captive who was not English shows little prejudice toward native Americans in the latter. Mary Jemison was born in 1742-1743 on board a ship sailing from Belfast Ireland to America. Her parents were Scotch-Irish and the interviewer and writer of her narrative noted she still had some Irish accent in her English speech at the time he took down her account when she was then about eighty years old.

The Jemison's were living on a farm located some ten miles north of present day Gettysburg Pennsylvania when on, Apr. 5th, 1758, they were set upon by a party of six Shawnees and four French. Mary's mother and father, her two brothers, a sister and some visitors there were killed. Mary and a young boy, a visitor, were taken away captive. On her way with these initial captors, they passed through a Shawnee town where she "saw a number of heads, arms, legs and other fragments of the bodies of some white people who had just been burnt…the whole appearance afforded a spectacle so shocking that even to this day, my blood almost curdles in my veins when I think of them." {45 Jemison p.74 & Passim}

After much travel she was brought to a Senaca village where she was adopted by a Senaca woman within the first year of captivity. She noted, "I was very fortunate in falling into their hands; for they were good natured women, peaceable and mild in their dispositions; temperate and gentle towards me. I have great reason to respect them, though they have been dead a great number of years."

The Senaca women gave Mary a new name, Dickewamis, which remained her name till death.

It was not long after her adoption in that first year that the possibility of redemption of Mary arose while the Indians she was with were at Fort Pitt. The adopter women on one occasion sensed this and quickly fled from Fort Pitt with Mary by canoe.

In 1760, two years after capture, a Dutchman, John Van Sice who frequented the Senaca village " of Genishaw" saw an opportunity to get hold of Mary intending to get the King's bounty for a redeemed captive. Mary became aware of his plan, and while working in the corn field one day, she saw him approaching her. She jumped up, ran from him and fled to a different town where she hid for three days. When the Senaca chiefs realized what the situation was, they told Mary she would not be redeemed without her consent. Mary's strong opposition to redemption would seem to indicate a lack of prejudice against the Indians even before her capture, as well as a total absence of any wording indicating such prejudice in her narrative.

Jemison does recount many of the cruelties of the Senaca toward captives brought to the village over the years. At one time, her adoptive sisters invited her to join them in viewing the torture of a prisoner, considered an exciting spectacle by them. But their mother hearing of this scolded the sisters for thinking of enjoying the torture, which she condemned, asking them how they would feel if it were their brother so tortured. They did not attend the event.

Soon Mary was matched up to a Lenape Indian man then living in the village; his name was Sheninjee. "The idea of my spending my days with him, at first seemed perfectly irreconcilable to my feelings [understandable, he was not her choice, but not necessarily showing a prejudice toward an Indian] but his good nature, generosity, tenderness and friendship toward me, soon gained my affection and strange as it may seem, I loved him." After Sheninjee died, Mary married another Indian his name was Hiokatoo, a Senaca, a much older man who died of consumption at about the age of 103. He was kind and loving to her, but "as a warrior, cruelties to his enemies perhaps were unparalleled and will not admit a word of palliation". It is said he "ever seemed to possess an unconquerable will that the Cherokees might be utterly destroyed". This per the writer of Mary's narrative, James E. Seaver.

Jemison notes on Senaca cruelties and kindness - "Notwithstanding all that has been said against the Indians, in consequence of their cruelties to there enemies- cruelties that I have witnessed and had abundant proof of, it is a fact that they are naturally kind, tender and peaceable toward their friends and strictly honest...No people can live more happy than the Indians in times of peace ,[I must interject here , those times of peace were only brief for the Senaca and the other Hodosonee, the so called Five Nations or Iroquois] before the introduction of spirituous liquors amongst them. Their lives were a constant round of pleasures. Their wants were few and easily satisfied and their cares were only for today; the bounds of calculations for future comfort not extending to the incalculable uncertainties of tomorrow."-- "the moral conduct of the Indians was uncontaminated. Their fidelity was perfect and was proverbial; they were strictly honest; they despised deception and falsehood; and chastity was held in high veneration and violation of it was considered sacrilege." Some of these words are surely Seaver's The pen of Seaver seems to have stretched Mary's wording to a higher level of perfection than I believe even she would have expressed, which is inconsistent with Seaver's pro -American bias. Still, surely much of it is Mary's feelings. Seaver was anti-Indian and pro-American per one editor of the narrative and that it cannot be known how closely his words fit Jemison's expressed words. However he did pass on much praise of the Indians.

Jemison remembered her adoptive sisters and mother with fondness and affection long after she moved away from them with her husband even though, as she notes, they had long since passed on. She also reflected on her Indian "brother", Kaujisetaugeau- "During the time that I lived in the family with him, he never offered the most trifling abuse; ...his whole conduct toward me was strictly honorable. I mourned his loss [death] as that of a tender brother, and shall recollect him through life with emotions of friendship and gratitude."

By 1777, four of the six Hodosonee tribes, including the Senaca had been convinced to help the British against the colonists. In 1779 a large colonial army of 3000 under General Sullivan swept through the Senaca towns dispersing the Senaca and destroying their crops, including their apple orchards.

Jemison, with hatred toward those attackers, determined to take her family (now having children) and withdraw to Gardow flats where they could safely dwell. Gardow flats was located "east of modern Castile

N.Y.". {46 Pecham p.75} This was outside of a strictly Senaca community, and it was here that she had contact with English speaking people and where she was contacted to relate her life to Dr. James Seaver.

Seaver does try to excuse Jamisen's praises thusly- " The vices of the Indians, she appeared disposed not to aggravate, and seemed to take pride in extolling their virtues. A kind of family pride inclined her to withhold whatever would blot the character of her descendants, and perhaps induced her to keep back many things that would have been interesting." Actually, he passed on a good number of Mary's descriptions of Indian atrocities. However, he is making a reasonable explanation for Mary's apparent great affection of Indian life, which if fully accepted could cause an unlimited diminution of her praise of Indian life. However, her free choices made throughout the years are entirely consistent with her apparent affection for her Indian life.

Mary was really won over to the native life and never stopped being an Indian, even after there was somewhat of a collapse of the Senaca tribe. The affection she received from her adopters overcame whatever feelings she must have had towards her captors who killed and scalped her original family.

It would seem that, before her capture, she had little prejudice towards the Indians which allowed her to readily accept her new life.

Seaver writes "...and notwithstanding her children and associates were all Indians, yet it was found that she possessed an uncommon share of hospitality...Her house was the strangers home; from her table the hungry were refreshed- she made the naked as comfortable as her means would admit of... She was the protector of the homeless fugitive..."

Later, after her relation to Seaver, Mary moved to a fully Indian community at Buffalo Creek Reservation where she died in 1833, ninety years old. {47 Peckham p.77}

Jemison may have possessed from birth a warm, generous nature, but her recorded behavior was really like what she experienced in her life with the Indians, but Seaver doesn't see the connection.

Chapter Nine

✦

Land Acquisitions

Mary Rowlandson, like Mary Jemison, had little ability to write a narrative, and both were solicited to recite their stories to educated writers. Rowlandson's writer has never been identified, and it was common at that time and place for writers to neglect or avoid identifying themselves. It seems likely, however that it was a minister as they were all educated and well able to write. Rowlandson's writer may be the Rev. William Hubbard who met Mary and her husband the Rev. Joseph Rowlandson shortly after her redemption as they passed each other on the road to Ipswich. Hubbard wrote the only account of King Philip's War authorized and paid for by Mass. Bay. Wording concerning the chaste treatment of Mary by her captors appears almost identical in his history published in 1676 and Mary's narrative published in 1682.

Rowlandson never noted any cruelty toward captives. That does not mean it did not occur elsewhere during King Philip's War; however, little is specified in any of the well-noted accounts of the war. Historian Jill LePore has uncovered a number of atrocities that occurred during Indian attacks as related in personal letters of colonists. Jemisen saw and heard of many cruelties over a period of at least two decades. Rowlandson was only "eleven weeks and five days…" with Indians, but length of time with Indians was not as important as the past experiences of the particular Indians one is with. The terrible battles and wars in which the Senaca and many other tribes, especially the Hodosonee (Iroquois) tribes, had been involved and recorded in over a period of nearly two centuries had a violent effect on those tribes. We do not have a history of intense battles involving the Narragansetts or the Wampanoag, only the Nipmuck and some Massachusetts had known previous intense fighting and that was with the Mohawk/Hodosonee in 1669. In all probability, repeated battles and killings develop vengeful mentalities in the surviving fighters and their cultures.

Rowlandson's deep prejudice prevented or limited her from recognizing or at least acknowledging decency by the Indians or any appreciation of the Indians' desire to use violence against the English. The only clear exception was her expression about her "master", Quanapin. Quanapin "seemed to me the best friend that I had of an Indian both in cold and hunger." Quanapin had abundant reason to resent the English well before the attack upon the Narragansetts in December. English acquisitions of the lands of the Narragansetts was causing troubles and surely the Indians could not even realize how outrageous were the true extent of lands which the English considered they owned. One deed, centered around Warwick R.I., dated Jan.12th 1642 supposedly conveys land reaching from Greenwich Bay westward for twenty miles (the width of present R.I.) with the north and south bounds vague. The deed is supposedly by Miantonomi, the "supreme sachem", and given to several Englishmen for 144 fathom of wampumpeage "with ffree and joynt consent of the present inhabitants being natives." Since at least four villages (Pawtuxet, Coweset, Shawomet and Potowomut) probably fell within those bounds, "the present inhabitants" after 1642 lived on land that no longer was theirs per that deed. It should be suspected that none of those inhabitants ever thought that the land they and their ancestors dwelt upon for times unknown was some how owned by some Englishmen.

Roger Williams received a grant of land from the previous "supreme sachem", Canonicus, which was about "14,000 acres of land"{48 Bicknell p.242}. Williams wrote that his grant of land in 1638 was somewhat limited by the existence of " Indians at Mashapog [Auburn R.I.], Notakunkunet [Notakunkunet Hill] and Pawtucket...".{49 Bicknell p.241} In 1677 Williams wrote in regards to a dispute between himself and William Harris with others, "As to my selling to them Pawtuxet and Providence: It is not true that I was such a fool to sell either of them, especially as W.H.(arris)[a vulgar rendering of William Harris] saith 'like a Halter in a market who gives most'". {50 Bicknell p.117} But we should believe the Indians were worse fools!

Our local histories and registries of deeds are filled with documents that show sales of native land to colonists. Were any of these not bogus? How can it be determined where possession of those native lands did pass in a truly just manner from any Indian who even had some type of "right" to transfer possession? Where was there a full understanding of what "sale" meant (the giving up of something entirely and forever unless or until it could be bought back), and was a sale done under fear or concern of what rejecting such sale might entail?

It is rare when we can quote Indian words that express negativity toward the sale of lands. It was never in the interest of the Europeans to mention Indian resistance to proposed sales or complaints about past land sales, except when one European group criticized another European group. But read these two records of such resistance; one by an apparent Abenacki chief in 1752, addressing one Capt. Stevens, deputy of the Mass. Bay Governor dealing with land in northern New England. A speech taken down at the time and relayed to the Governor, that has somehow survived.

"Speech of the Abenakis of St. Francois to Capt. Stevens, deputy from the Governor of Boston, in presence of M. leBaron de Longueuil, Gov. of Canada, and of Iroquois from the Sault St. Louis and from the lake of the Two Mountains, on the 5th of July 1752. Arti-aneto, Chief Orator:"

" Brother,
"We shall talk to you as if we were speaking to your Governor in Boston. We hear on all sides that this Governor and the Bostonnais say the Abenakis are bad people. It is in vain that you charge us with bad hearts; it is always you, our brothers who have attacked us; you have a sweet tongue, but a heart of gall. I admit, that when you begin it we can defend ourselves.
"We tell you brother, that we are not anxious for war. We like nothing better than to be at peace, and it needs only that our English brothers keep peace with us ...We wish to keep possession of the lands on which we live... We will not give up an inch of land we inhabit, beyond that long ago decided upon by our brothers... We forbid you absolutely from killing

a single beaver or taking one bit of wood on our lands. If you want the wood we will sell it to you, but you shall not have it without our permission.

Who has authorized you to have our lands measured ? We pray the governor of Boston to have these surveyors punished, for we cannot believe they are acting under his orders. You are then the arbiters of peace between us. As soon as you cease to encroach upon these lands, we shall be at peace.

"Our father here present [the Canadian Governor] has nothing to do with what we are saying to you [surely the French prepared or helped to prepare the whole speech]. It is on our own behalf and for our allies that we speak. We regard our father simply as a witness of our words ...Under no pretext whatever are you to pass beyond your limits...We are a free people; allies of the French king from whom we have received our Religion, and help in time of need".{51 Baker p.337}

A second record, is of a letter by Philip in the late 1660's. Philip, "the sly fox" as Mary Rowlandson called him, cleverly tries to use the Plymouth government's opposition to too rapid land grabs by greedy colonists, by using the common period of seven years, so often used in English law, to at least halt English acquisitions temporarily, perhaps while conspiring for a permanent solution, war.

This undated letter, found in " Collections of Massachusetts Historical Society." ii40 written by "Philip's aide".

" To the much honored Gov. Mr. Thomas Prince dwelling at Plymouth.

"King Philip desire to let you understand that he could not come to the court, for Tom his interpreter, has a pain in his back, that he could not travel so far, and Philip sister is very sick. Philip would entreat that favor of you, and any of the magistrates, if any English or Engians speak about any land, he pray you to give them no answer at all. This last summer he made that promise with you that he would not sell no land in 7 years time, for that he would have no English trouble him before that time, he has not for got that you promise him. He will come a sune as possible he can speak with you, and so I rest.

Your very loving friend
Philip P
dwelling at mount hope neck"{52 Drake,B of I book 3 p.14}

The question this letter generates is why would the so-called "supreme Wampanoag sachem" need to ask anyone to promise to not allow purchases of Wampanoag land? The answer must be that Philip knew he could not control, without the help of the government of Plymouth, the manipulations used by the English.

While I do maintain that a true conveyance of the possession of land by natives was something unlikely to happen, trade by individual Indians happened regularly. Natives did trade for many things such as pots, pans, hatchets, hoes, cloaks, stockings, blankets and the unmentionable: guns, lead and powder. Anything that might empower Indians (guns, boats, horses) was made illegal, but the Indians got them anyway, undoubtedly by trade. The natives in the early years traded furs (until the supply was depleted). Later, wampum was used as money both by natives and Europeans with which the natives could buy English goods and the English could buy native goods including land – land which the "seller" didn't really possess.

The land acquisitions by the English and the eventual implementation of the rights of ownership were arguably the most basic causes of King Philip's war. But the immediate cause in the case of the Narragansetts joining the war was the English invasion of their country, starting with the destruction of the villages, killings and captures in the Greenwich Bay area. Those aggressive acts plus other previous offenses, gave Quanapin and the Narragansetts plenty of reasons to truly hate Englishmen.

Chapter Ten

✦

Mary Meets Philip

After the burning of the deserted Indian village Mary Rowlandson's 6th remove was to an area near present Northfield. After two days of travel, they reached the deserted English town of Squaukheag, where they fed off of the English fields. Here there came an Indian with a basket of horse liver. Mary asked him for a piece of it. He asked her would if she would eat it. She answered yes, and he gave her a piece which she tried to cook upon a fire. Someone stole "half of it" before she could cook it, whereupon she devoured the remainder raw. This incident demonstrates how almost everyone was out for whatever food he could acquire, even by theft; yet some were ready to share what little they had even with a captive. Mary notes, "That night we had a mess of wheat for our Supper."

The next day, they traveled up the east side of the Connecticut River where Mary's son, Joseph came to visit her while she rested. They continued up the river until night (South Vernon Vt.).In the morning, they crossed the river where they intended to join or meet with Philip's group. When Mary reached the other side of the river, a large number of those Indians gathered about her - "I observed they asked one another questions and laughed and rejoiced over their Gains and Victories... I fell to weeping which was the first time to my remembrance , that I weep before them. ...There one of them asked me, why I wept, I could hardly tell what to say : yet I answered, they would kill me. No, said he, none will hurt you. Then came one of them and gave me two spoonfuls of Meal to comfort me, and another gave me half a pint of Pease...". Mary was a curiosity to this new group of Indians but their treatment of her was kindly.

Then Mary was taken to "see King Philip, he bade me to come in and sit down. And asked me whether I woold smoke... During my abode in this place, Philip spake to me to make a shirt for his boy, which I did, for which he gave me a shilling: I offered the money to my master, but he bade me to keep it: and with it I bought a piece of Horse flesh."

Here we see an example of Algonquin reciprocation which is something like buying and selling but essentially it is giving a gift or favor in return for another's gift or favor or kindness. The English never seemed to view gifts from Indians in the same manner as the Indians did. Quanapin would not take the money, perhaps because he knew Philip had given it in reciprocation for the favor of the shirt, and not as a payment for the shirt.

"Afterwards he [Philip] asked me to make a Cap for his boy, for which he invited me to Dinner. I went, and he gave me a Pan-cake, about as big as two fingers...I thought I never tasted pleasanter meat in my life. There was a Squaw who spake to me to make a shirt for her Sannup [her mate].for which she gave me a piece of Bear. Another asked me to knit a pair of Stockins, for which she gave me a quart of Pease..." Here we see their recognition of Mary's talent for sewing and knitting. Also we see reciprocal acts.

It doesn't seem as though her master's household is providing her with much food, but Mary is not treated as a slave or even as a servant from what we read in her narrative.

One captive, Mary Thurston of Medfield gave Mary a hat but the squaw who owned Thurston took the hat away from Mary. At another place- "Here was the Squaw that gave me one spoonful of Meal. I put it in my Pocket to keep it safe: yet notwithstanding somebody stole it, but put five Indian Corns in the room of it...". Was this reciprocation for a theft ?

Chapter Eleven

✦

Careless Captors

Not only were many Indians often kind to captives but they were careless in keeping them captive. The Indians who had sojourned with Philip at Sagihock near Albany N.Y. had had an English captive who escaped and carried intelligence to Gov. Andros. He told Andros that there was a large body of non New England Indians that Philip could well have been soliciting to join in his cause. Andros, who had stood aside from this war between New England Indians and New England English, was willing to see the Puritans stressed and weakened by the war. We saw how he attempted to use the war as a means to take control of part of the Connecticut colony back in July and how he was rebuffed then. He was more successful on eastern Long Island. Using the same excuse there, he took a measure of control of the Puritan towns on the eastern end of the island. Now he saw a danger of a larger, expanding uprising of Algonquin tribes dwelling from New York to Virginia, a real threat to all English America. As a good steward of the King and the Duke of York, he had to work against Philip, even if it helped the Puritans. Andros solicited the Kanyenkehake (called Mohawks by the Algonquin and English) to attack Philip's party at Sagihock. {53Jennings p.314, /N.Y. Colonial Documents} Not only did the Mohawks attack in New York, but their war parties kept up raids throughout New England on its' Indians continually and long after the demise of Philip. Philip's attempt at gaining the help of western and northern Algonquins, and possibly the Mohawks themselves, instead brought on the dreaded Mohawks against him. Without the intelligence provided by the escaped captive, would some of those Algonquins have joined in Philip's cause before the move of the Mohawks made such assistance a threat to the tenuous peace between those Algonquins and the Mohawks? The Mohawks with the western Hodosonee had just finished a long war of attrition against the Susquehannahock whom they finally subdued. While that conflict went on, the Mohawks perhaps would not have taken on Philip's party , but by 1675 they were ready. Small Mohawk and other Hodosonee raids on the New England Indians were then acceptable. Philip was certainly not ready to retaliate. Gov. Thomas Dongan of New York would one day remark, " New England in their last Warr with the Indians had been ruined, had not Sir Edmond Andros sent some of those Nations [Hodosonee] to their assistance."{54 Jennings p.314/N.Y. Col. Doc. III, 393}

Another case of intelligence provided by escaped captives, this one more limited in effect occurred when John Gilbert and Ed. Steblin escaped in May 1676 from an encampment near Turner's Falls and told of that encampment, also informing that most of the Indians there were women and children. A force of more than 150 men from three Conn. River towns, knowing of the location, "marched silently in the dead of Night May 18 and came upon...Indians...whom they found almost in a dead Sleep...marching up, they fired amain into the very Wigwams, killing many... and frightened others...[which] made them run into the River...down a steep Fall, they perished...-When first awakened, [by] the Thunder of their Guns, they cried out Mohawks, Mohawks".{55 Hubbard 229-230} This alarm caused by fear of Mohawks here and in a couple of other references shows how frightened the New England Indians were of surprise raids by Mohawks.

One can wonder if these Indians ever realized how dangerous it was to have captives escape when their own situation depended upon hiding from their enemies in order to prevent such enemies from locating their encampment. Nothing served the English combat efforts better than the raiding of a weakly protected encampment.

Chapter Twelve

✦

"he shewed me the way"

On Mary's ninth removal, they moved up the Connecticut River five miles where they crossed to the west side. "…here lived a sorry Indian, who spoke to me to make him a shirt. When I had done it, he would pay me nothing. But he living by the River side, where I often went to fetch water, I would be putting him to mind, and calling for my pay: [Mary wants "pay", not reciprocation] at last he told me if I would make another shirt, for a Papoos not yet born, he would give me a knife, which he did... I carried the knife in, and my master asked me to give it to him, and I was not a little glad that I had anything that they would accept of, and be pleased with". Surely a captive should not be given a knife. It appears from Mary's words that the "sorry Indian" was a resident of that place and not of the hostiles. Also note Mary's assertiveness with that Indian.

"My Son being now about a mile from me, I asked liberty to go and see him, they bade me go, and away I went: but Quickly lost myself, traveling over Hills and through Swamps, and could not find the way to him. And I cannot but admire at the wonderful power and goodness of God to me, in that , though I was gone from home, and met with all sorts of Indians, and those I had no knowledge of, and there being no Christian soul near me; yet not one of them offered the least imaginable miscarriage to me. I turned homeward again, and met with my master, he shewed me the way to my Son."

Again, Mary gave credit to God, and, apparently without contemplating it, to herself, for the respectful behavior of those Indians. Also, it may be that Quanapin had concern for her and took the time and effort to find Mary, bring her to her son and perhaps lead her back.

Although Mary's words here do not show appreciation for or pleasure at Quanapin's help, later on we will see expressions of great admiration of him, and God gets no mention, a great exception.

Why would the sachem seek out Mary and take her to her son, and why would none of the Indians she met alone in the forest offer her the "least miscarriage"? Well, this was not exceptional behavior for Indians; rather it was the norm, at least for this part of the world and for this time in history. In particular, Indian men in all the narratives reviewed , (with the exception of some tribes in the western United States), never abuse or take advantage of female captives regardless of opportunity.

Mary Jamisen was fifteen years old when she and one younger boy traveled for days after capture with several Shawnee captors with no hint of abuse by them.

Sarah Gilbert, nineteen with brother Ben Gilbert Jr., eleven, and one male captor, were set off on a trail separate from the other captives for several days and she was untouched. Elizabeth Gilbert, mother of the captured Gilbert family, about fifty-five at the time of capture, during the journey with the captors was allowed to fall behind because she could not keep up. An Indian of the group fell back to her and warned her that she would perish if she did not keep up. He, being on a horse, rode on but soon returned to her and put her on the horse and so allowed her to continue. Very much like Mary Rowlandson this Elizabeth gave God the credit for the softening of the Indian's heart. This was at the time of the Revolutionary War, May 1780.{56 Gilbert p.52} Another daughter, Elizabeth, twelve when she was adopted by the Cayuga/Hodosonee Indians, who after her release "always retained an affection towards her Indian father, called John Huston", one of the captors. "She remembered his kindness to her when in captivity." After her release and return to Pennsylvania she met some Indians who knew Huston, whereupon she sent presents to him by them. One of the 15 captives was killed during their journey to Indian country, it should be noted. {57 Gilbert-Vaughan p.181}

Quintin Stockwell was captured on Sept. 19, 1677 from Deerfield, Mass. by a party of Norwattucks, a Connecticut River tribe, plus one Narragansett. He and twenty others were taken northward where captives were traded, often to the French. Stockwell says the Indian who first took him was, according to the Indian captain there, the worst of the captors, but that captain "Ashpelon...was all along very kind to me, and a great comfort to the English". Stockwell says "the horses stolen at Hatfield and Deerfield were used to carry the women". Despite the "kind" treatment by the captain, some captives received abuses by some Indians, and Stockwell's life was threatened often. {58 Baker p.111}

Col. John Smith was eighteen when captured by two Lenape and one Cansatauga in May 1755. He was adopted later, living with Indians from 1755 to 1759. Smith observed that, in times when there was plenty of food and the men were not at war- "They appear to be fulfilling the scriptures beyond those who profess to believe in them, in that they take no thought for tomorrow, and also in living in love, peace and friendship together without disputes."{59 Drake I.C. p.205} Further he states, "From [the time of his adoption] ...I never knew them to make any distinction between me and themselves whatever... if we scarce of provisions, we all shared one fate."{60 Ibid p.205}

Chapter Thirteen

✦

Abuses of Captives

There were many reports of abuse of captives by the Indians.

John Gyles, captured in 1689 near Pemaquid Maine at the age of ten, was with Indian allies of the French, mostly with the Maliseets of New Brunswick and Nova Scotia, for six years. He notes "A captive among the Indians is exposed to all manner of abuse and to the upmost tortures unless his master or some of his master's relations lay down a ransom...by which they may redeem them from their cruelties.... The priest [Fr. Simon Du la Place, a Recollet missionary with the Maliseets] of this river [Penobscot] ... In his sermons he most severely reprehended the Indians for their barbarities to the captives. He would often tell them that excepting their errors in religion the English were a better people than themselves."{61 Gyles p.93} One of Gyles brothers was "most barbarously tortured to death by the Indians."{62 Gyles p.93} Gyles himself was tortured numerous times, once by Micmacs (natives of northern New Brunswick) who visited his captors. These Indians had had relatives killed by English fishermen, and he was apparently tortured to avenge their murdered relatives. Gyles said his master and squaw had sometimes hidden him from likely tormentors.

The story of John Gyles may be self written. A number of others that follow were either written or edited by the Rev. Cotton Mather (1663-1703). Mather's message, in all of these stories wherein he had a hand, was, firstly, that the English were being punished by God for their slacking off from religion. Secondly, when captives received any favor during captivity, it was by God's hand and that should prompt thanksgiving and a return to proper observances. Throughout, there is a running diatribe of Indians, but that part, I submit, is not part of the religious lesson, rather it is there to display, or to create a display of the depravity of the Indian, and generate contempt or hatred of them.

Mather wrote about captives taken from Salmon Falls, New Hampshire. On Mar.18, 1690 a French and Indian war party of about fifty struck Salmon Falls. Nearly thirty English were slain there and about fifty taken captive and led to Canada. This was at least partially done for promised French bounty. An Indian known as Hope Hood, apparently annoyed by the crying of five year old James Kay while on the journey to Canada, took the child, stripped and scourged him. The child continued to cry, and at some point, Hope Hood took the child and forced one of his eyes out of its' socket. Later when the child, exhausted, stopped moving on, Hope Hood then sank his hatchet into the child's head, chopped up his body and threw the parts into the river.{63 C. Mather p.139}

Mary Ferguson was also captured at Salmon Falls. Her account tells of a girl of fifteen, burdened with a heavy load who, at one point "bursts into tears", whereupon her master chopped off her head, scalped the head and then "he ran about laughing and bragging...showing the scalp to the rest."{64 C.Mather p.143}

Mary Plaisted was captured about three weeks after the birth to her of a male child. On the trail north, she grew exhausted and sat down on the trail. Her master took the baby from her and swung the child by the legs smashing the child's head against a tree and then threw the body into a river. {65 Baker p.78}

Hannah Dustin, colonial heroine, was taken in Mar. 1697; she had just given birth to her eighth child. Shortly after starting their trek to Canada, "they dashed out the brains of the infant against a tree.". Several of the other captives, as they began to tire, were dispatched by the captors. Dustin's mid-wife was also captured at that time. Mather was willing to admit some kindness by the captors as long as he could ascribe it to God i.e. "the good God who hath all hearts in his hands, heard the sighs of these prisoners [Dustin's group] and gave them to find unexpected favor from the master who laid claim to them." Dustin, Mary Neff (the mid -wife) and "an English youth," Samuel Lenorson, "together found opportunity one night while the Indians that held them slept, to pick up loose hatchets and did set about hatcheting ten of the twelve Indians. The Indians consisted of two adult men, two squaws and six children, one child and one squaw escaped. They cut off the scalps of the ten [eight], after their return to home they received 50 pounds from the General Assembly..." for their exploit.{66 C. Mather p.162-164}

The Rev. John Williams, his family of eight, and forty other English were taken captive from Deerfield Mass. in 1703 by a body of Catholic Mohawks and French. They were to be led to Canada with the plan to have them adopted by either French or Indian families. The total number of prisoners taken at two towns that day was 112; 16 were killed on the march and two died of starvation. At that time Williams owned a Negro man and his wife as slaves "The Redeemed Captive" (found in Vaughan) by Rev. Williams with some participation by Cotton Mather tells not only of the many killings by captors, but also of many contrasting kindnesses . He writes, just after leaving Deerfield "they killed a suckling child of the English". In the first "night an Englishman made his escape, in the morning I was called for and ordered by the general to tell the English, that if any more made their escape, they would burn the rest of the prisoners." {67 J. Williams p.174} When William's wife faltered on the journey "the cruel and bloodthirsty savage who took her, slew her with his hatchet..." Further on, Williams writes "they killed another suckling infant...and before night, a girl of about eleven years of age ....the journey was long and tedious, we traveled with such speed that four women were tired and then slain by them...a girl of four was killed by her ...master...the snow being so deep...that he could not carry the child and his pack too."

The decencies of captors noted by the Reverend are often attributed to God's help such as "... yet their savage cruel tempers were so overruled by God that they did not kill him [William's four year old son], but in their pity he was spared...that [they] carried or drawed him on sleighs... . My youngest daughter, age seven, was carried all the journey and looked after with a great deal of tenderness... . My son Samuel [fifteen] and my eldest daughter [thirteen] were pitied so as to be drawn on sleighs when unable to travel."{68 J. Williams p.176-179}

"We traveled not far on the first day, God made the heathen so to pity our children that, though they had several wounded persons of their own to carry upon their shoulders for thirty miles...yet they carried our children, incapable of traveling, upon their shoulders and in their arms." {69 J. Williams p.174}

It can be thought that at least some of the kindnesses were motivated by the desire to bring back healthy captives for adoption.

The Rev. Williams hardly refers to his daughter, Eunice who we know from other sources married an Indian and refused repeated and persistent attempts to repatriate her, even when she returned for a visit to New England. She died at the Catholic/Mohawk town of Caughnawaga at age of ninety. {70 Baker p.139-153}

Mather writes of Robert Rogers, one of those captured at Salmon Falls in Mar.1690, later briefly escaping and then recaptured. In an apparent lesson to others, he is burnt by his Abenaki captors in front of the other captives. Chunks of his flesh were cut out if him and then thrown at him. He soon perished from this torture. {71 C.Mather p.138}

Mehitable Goodwin was taken captive with her child of only five months age, from their home on the coast of Maine in about 1690. Her captors took her infant from her arms and smashed its' brains out. {72 C. Mather p.140,141}

Hannah Swarton was taken captive when Casco Fort was assaulted and taken by Indians in 1690. She or Mather wrote that she was often threatened with death if she didn't keep up on the trail. The one other English captive with Hannah was killed because she could not or would not keep up. The Indians told Hannah that the eldest of her four children had been killed by them shortly after his capture. {73 C. Mather p.148-150} After near nine months traveling with Indians, she passed over to the French from whom she was redeemed in Nov. 1695. Two of her children who were also captured became converted to Catholicism and remained in Canada.

In the excerpts from these last nine captivity stories Cotton Mather appears to be either the true author or editor of others' stories. Those stories had similar insults and atrocities committed by the Indians. In those stories, there was little about considerate behavior by captors, From this and more extensive reading of Cotton I suspect accuracy was sacrificed to suit Cotton's agenda.

Chapter Fourteen

◆

Decent Captors

Other sources present stories from returned captives of more positive Indian behavior .

For example, Sylvanus Johnson was taken captive at the time of the French and Indian Wars and was later redeemed. He lived later in Walpole, New Hampshire where he was said to be an "honest and upright man". It is said that he actually regretted being redeemed and that the Indians he spent his youth with were "morally superior" to the English.

The Rev. Jonathan Curtis wrote a narrative for Isabella M'Coy of Epson, New Hampshire captured "probably in 1747". Of her journey to Canada, he notes - "The kindness she received from them [her captors] was far greater than she had expected from those who were often distinguished for their cruelties. Nothing like insult or indecency did they ever offer her during the whole time she was with them." {74 Curtis /Calloway p.19}

Elizabeth Hanson (1684-1737) was taken into captivity on Aug. 27,1724, fourteen days after the birth of a child, and carried away with four of her children from their home in Dover Township, New Hampshire. One editor of Hanson's narrative, "God's Mercy Surmounting Man's Cruelty..."might have been Samuel Bownas, a Quaker preacher from old England.{75 Hanson p.230} The notable aspect of this narrative, 1st pub. in 1728, is the contrast between the Quaker woman's attitude towards the Indians and the bigotry of most Puritan narratives. Although she does often ascribe restraint by her captors as from God's, grace as do the Puritans, she is often surprisingly willing to credit any Indian when credit seems due. Two of her children were killed at the home site,- one as a "warning" and another because he kept screaming "and the Indians, to ease themselves of the noise and to prevent the danger of a discovery [by the absent men] that might arise from it...knocked its brains out." After that they quickly began their journey north. "The [Indian] captain, though he had as great a load as he could well carry and was helped up [upon his back?], did for all that carry my babe for me in his arms, which I took as a favor from him." This same Indian "...when we came at very bad places he would push me up before him. In all which he showed some humanity and civility...I was secretly thankful to God as the moving cause thereof."

One of Elizabeth's daughters and her particular master divided-off from Elizabeth's party and after some time of their journey "...my daughter's master being sick was not able to hunt for flesh. Neither had they any corn in that place but were forced to eat bark of trees for a whole week."

"Being almost famished in this distress, Providence ordered that some other Indians, hearing of their misery and want, came to visit them (these people being kind and helpful to one another which is very commendable) and brought them the guts and liver of a beaver which afforded them a good repast, being but four in number, the Indian, his wife and daughter and my daughter".{76 Ibid p230-235}

Note both credit to Indians and to Providence here.

Later, Elizabeth's group stopped at an Indian "fort" where they were received with "great rejoicing...shouting, drinking and feasting..." . It appears, however, it was still the responsibility of her master to hunt for his group's needs of game. He was gone "about a week" but returned empty-handed in ill humor and irrational, threatening Elizabeth and daughter by his behavior. Elizabeth fled to "another wigwam" where her master's mother-in-law came in and "brought a small skin to cover my feet withall, informing me that my master intended now to kill us..." Elizabeth protested to the old squaw "... that in his absence I had been diligent to do as I was ordered by him. Thus as well as I could, I made her sensible how unreasonable he was. Now though she could not understand me nor I her, but by signs, we reasoned as well as we could. She therefore makes signs that I must die, advising me by pointing up with her fingers in her way, to pray to God, endeavoring by her signs and tears to instruct me in that which was most needful, viz. to prepare for death which now threatened me. The poor old squaw was so very kind and tender to me that she would not leave me all that night but laid herself down at my feet, designing [in her thoughts?] what she could to assuage her son-in-law's wrath, who had conceived evil against me chiefly, as I understood, because the want of victuals urged him to it."{77 Ibid p.236}

The next day, her master set off hunting again- "He had been gone but a little till returned...having shot some wild duck..." They all fed freely of ducks, and her master's mode lightened; with no more threats by him, Elizabeth's "spirits were a little easier". Note here, the old squaw saw Elizabeth not as a Puritan, not as a Quaker, not as a usurper, not inferior, not superior but as another human being suffering under threat of death. She did all she could to mitigate Elizabeth's distress. Nor was it just the old squaw who feared the master's display of wrath; his wife and daughter "broke out in a great crying" when he angrily and begrudgingly threw a corn cob at Elizabeth that day.{78 Ibid p.238}

After about five months among the Indians Elizabeth was sold to the French. She was finally ransomed or exchanged to the English, returning home on Sept.1, 1725, having had two children killed by the Indians both on the day of the attack.{79 Ibid p.242}

At the age of five Francis Slocum was taken captive in the summer of 1778 from her home at what is now Wilkes-Barre Penn. by three Delawares and was later adopted. She effectively became an Indian living and traveling with them. In 1835, a white man traveling by stopped at the Indian village, "Dead Man's village", where Francis, her husband, Shepancanah and their children lived. The white man was permitted to stay in their cabin. The man, George Ewing, suspected Francis might be a white woman, and she finally admitted that she was. "She recollected that she had many brothers and sisters but assumed that they must be dead by now. That probably permitted her to speak now, because she had hitherto feared her relatives would come and take her away if they learned of her whereabouts. She had been happy with the Indians and distrusted the whites." When she was discovered and that fact revealed to her still living brothers and sisters they visited her and urged her to return to Pennsylvania. She declined saying, " I am happy here, I shall die here and lie in the graveyard, and they will raise the pole at my grave with the white flag on it , and the Great Spirit will know where to find me."{80 Peckham p.116-126}

Zadock Steele, at age twenty-one, was taken prisoner on Oct.17,1780 near Randolph Vt. by a group of mainly Caughanwagas (Catholic Mohawks). He wrote his own narrative of his captivity, at the close of which he wrote: "The savage when he does a deed of charity towards his prisoner, is no doubt less liable to be actuated by a selfish principle and influenced to hope of reward or by a fear of losing his reputation, than he is who [as a Christian, Jew etc., perhaps] has been made acquainted with the gracious reward offered to those who 'do unto others as they would that others should do unto them' and knows the bitter consequences of the contrary practice [hell?]."{81 Steele/ Calloway p.147}

Fanny Kelly, her husband and family were like many of the whites seeking better places to live in the west. She left us her "Narrative of My Captivity Among the Sioux Indians". She was taken captive in 1864 and brought to an Indian village where she dwelt for a considerable time. In one paragraph she gives us a window into the mind of Indians of that period. " This country seemed scarred by countless trails, where the Indian ponies have dragged lodge poles in the savages' change of camp or hunting. The hatred of the Indian for its' occupation [the land] by the white man is very bitter. The felling of timber, killing of Buffalo, traveling of a wagon train or any of permanent possession by the white man excites deadly hostility. It is the Indian's last hope, if they yield and give up, they will have to die or ever after be governed by the white man's laws...consequently they lose no opportunity to kill or steal from and harass the whites."{82 Kelly p.350} Kelly was a captive with the Sioux from May 12, 1864 to Dec. 12, of the same year. Compare this with the natives' attitudes at the close of King Philips' War when many thought they could adapt after surrender.

Recording her "Six weeks in the Sioux Tepees", Sarah Wakefield asserted that "the Indians were as respectful toward me as any white man would be toward a lady: and now, when I hear all the Indians abused, it aggravates me, for I know some are as manly , honest and noble as our race."{83 Wakefield p.42} Wakefield was under criticism for her defense of Indians and she is probably a little generous to the whites here in her wording. Her capture occurred after the Sioux uprising of 1863.

From these selections of captivity narratives, mostly of New England captivities, we can see both cruelties and kindnesses by captors. All these narratives were recited by or written by the captives themselves or by highly motivated editor/writers. With the possible exceptions of Mary Jamison or Francis Slocum none of them would appear liable to inflate, exaggerate or distort their comments in order to create an appreciation of Indian decency, while on the other hand they all could well bear antipathy toward their captors who must have brought on fear, stress, exhaustion etc. and, in some cases, the loss of loved ones.

Considering the above narratives and noting that all our histories are told by beneficiaries of the winning side of that history, one can still draw an assessment that there was charitableness and decency among the native peoples, despite what was then happening to them. That apparent decency occurred even without the teachings of the philosophers and preachers available to the Europeans.

As to the attractiveness of Indian life read these quotes;

Ben Franklin wrote: "The proneness of human Nature to a life of ease, of freedom from care and labour appears strongly in the little success that has hitheto attended every attempt to civilize our American Indians". Further on, Franklin comes up with an answer to his own musing on why societies ever gave up the simple, satisfying life such as the Indians seemed to enjoy: "...so I am apt to imagine that close Societies subsisting by Labour and Arts, arose first not from necessity. [but rather] When numbers being driven by war from their hunting grounds and prevented by seas or by other nations were crowded together in some narrow Territories, which without labour would not afford them food."{85 Franklin/Washburn p.61}

William Penn said of the Indians: "We sweat and toil, and toil to live, their pleasure feeds them, I mean their Hunting , Fishing and Fouling.-In this they are sufficiently revenged on us".

Crevecocur's editor writes - "As J. Hector Crevecocur summed it up in 1782 in his 'Letters From an American Farmer' – there must be something in their social bond something singularly captivating, and far superior to anything to be boasted of among us; for thousands of Europeans are Indians, and we have no examples of one of these Aborigines having from choice become Europeans."{86 N.Y. Times Mag. 1/31/1993}

Chapter Fifteen

✦

Injustice Recognized – But Used

Why could not any of the New England colonists see that they were all in the process of usurping these lands from the natives? Perhaps the answer for most was simple- they did not want to. To consider such would mean either giving up on new found treasure or accepting the guilt caused by recognizing the wrong doing; neither was acceptable.

Other English writers not so closely involved in those times and in later times had no trouble recognizing what was going on; it was pursuit of self- interest at others' expense.

Massachusetts Governor Thomas Hutchinson was a great-great grandson of Ann Hutchinson (a non conformist Puritan banished from Mass. Bay in 1638) and great grandson of Capt. Edward Hutchinson who was killed in K.P.'s War. Thomas wrote a history of Massachusetts, first published in 1774.{87 T. Hutchinson p. IX} In it he wrote: "We are to apt to consider the Indians as a race of beings by nature inferior to us, and born to servitude, Philip was a man of high spirit and could not bear to see the English of New Plymouth extending their settlements over the dominions of his ancestors and although his father had... conveyed to them all they were possessed of, [here he honors Plymouth's pretense] yet he had sense enough to distinguish a free voluntary covenant from one made under a sort of duress, and could never rest until he brought on the war which ended in his destruction."{88 T. Hutchinson p.241}

Royal Agent Edward Randolph (1632-1703) who investigated Mass. Bay's activities many times, wrote the following to William Penn in Nov.9, 1688: "This barbarous people, the Indians were never civilly treated by the late government [of Mass. Bay] who made it their business to encroach upon their lands and by degrees drive them out of all. That was the grounds and beginning of the last war." {89 T. Hutchinson p.93}

Historian Francis Jennings wrote of Rhode Island Gov. William Coddington's letter to Gov. Andros of July 21,1675: "a former magistrate of Mass. Bay (and a former Puritan), Coddington had no illusions about the honor of the oligarchs. The invader purpose [United Colonies upon the Narragansetts], he wrote had been 'to bring the Indians there to their own terms, and to call that part of Rhode Island theirs'." {90 Jennings p.307} As earlier, stated the right to conquered land by the United Colony due to their victory in the Great Swamp fight was nullified by the "Order of the Privy Council [essentially the King] Dec.13,1678" two years after King Philip's war.

In 1675 Capt. John Wynbourne wrote of his observations in the time his ship was in Boston harbor on the conduct of the Mass. Bay government. He was there three months. He made a report that was read to the Privy Council. Wynbourne judged that King Philip's War was brought on the by tyranny of Mass. Bay's government toward the Indians.

Edmond Andros was called back to London in 1677. At the Privy Council committee meeting on April 8, 1678, Andros testified that in his judgment Mass. Bay had caused the expansion of King Philip's War if it had not actually begun the war. Actually, it was Plymouth's actions towards Philip, not Mass. Bay's, that precipitated outbreak of the war.

Gov. Sir William Berkeley wrote to the government in England in April 1676. In his letter he blamed the New England colonies for King Philip's War (whom he claimed also caused the Indians of Virginia to go to war) because they had taken too much land from the natives. He wrote, "for the natives complained that [New England colonists] had left them no land to support and insure their wives and children from famine".{92 Webb p.205} I present Berkeley's words not because he had a specially accurate view of the cause of the war, but that he needed to present New England's leadership in a worst position than himself. At that time he was faced with Virginia's own Indian war and the start of Bacon's Rebellion. He chose to blame New England's troubles on New England's lust for and grasp of native land, because he knew it to be an obvious cause to the minds of those in old England. Berkeley was later deposed by the King and deported from Virginia on May 8, 1678.

Contrast the above opinions of these separate or non-involved English with the letter of Gov. Winslow of Plymouth to the Commissioners of the United Colonies of Sept.9, 1675, wherein he tries to totally absolve the Plymouth government from any blame regarding land acquisition as a cause of the present war. – " I think I can clearly say, that before these present troubles trouble broke out, the English did not possess one foot of Land in this Colony, but what was fairly obtained by honest purchase of the Indian Proprietors." {93 I. Mather "B.H" p146}.

Also this from Hubbard "...and [because] the Indians are easily prevailed upon with to part with their Lands, we first made a Law, that none should purchase or receive a Gift of any Land of the Indians without the knowledge of our Court, and Penalty of a Fine, five Pound per Acre for all that should be bought as [so] obtained."{94 Hubbard p.57} Such a law was important to the colonial government to keep control of land grabs, to prevent too much aggravation of the natives, to limit counterclaims by different English and to keep order. An indication of why the law served colonial purposes is obtained by considering the question,- what good would the fine do for the natives if the buyers do not have to give up the land, but only pay a fine to the colony, albeit a deterrent. Other colonial writers claim the natives were improvidently selling land, a convenient explanation for the land grabs.

When the imperative need of the poor English for land for subsistence is considered, when the lust for land by wealthy English for acquiring greater wealth is considered, and when the attitude of the leaders and the teachers are considered, any and all land dealings are suspect. As to the colonial attitudes, note the writings of two prominent colonial Englishmen of these times: Increase Mather and Daniel Gookin. Gookin was Major General or Commander-in-Chief of Mass. Bay's army in 1643, in his narrative, COLLECTIONS... he selected these psalms as justification for the colonist's actions: "Ask of me, and I shall give thee the heathen for thine inheritance, and the uttermost parts of the earth for thy possession"(Psalm ii8) and (Psalm lxxii8,9) "He shall have dominion also from sea to sea, and from the ends of the earth. They that live in the wilderness shall bow before him; and his enemies shall lick the dust." {95 Gookin "H.C." Vol. I title page} Gookin was in control of the so-called Praying Indians and this was a man disliked by many English colonists because he seemed too friendly with the Praying Indians.

This by I. Mather - " That the Heathen people amongst whom we live, and the Land the Lord God of our Fathers hath given to us for a rightful Possession, have at sundry times been plotting mischievous devices against that part of the English Israel which is seated in these going down of the Sun..." {96 I. Mather "B.H." p.89}

Slotkins, editor of Mather's "Brief Hist." wrote: "With his son Cotton [1663-1728], Increase [1639-1723] shaped the political program, as well as the philosophic-theological theory of the Puritan conservatives...". Increase was educated at Harvard and Trinity College in Dublin. {97 Slotkins p.55}

It was not just the acquisitiveness of the settlers or the use or misuse of religious writings that distorted the mentality of the English, it was also the expansionist policies, direct and indirect, of the government in England that allowed most settlers to dispossess the natives without ever questioning the immorality of the dispossession. England had been engaged in expansionist colonialism for one hundred years before 1675.

Quinn wrote: "...intermittently from about 1520 onward and less intermittently from the middle of the century, colonization of Ireland by new English settlers had been considered as one way...of solving for good and all the problem of ruling the Irish."{98 Quinn p.106} There had been invasions and settlements in Ireland since the 12th century but colonization as a means of control began in the 16th century and the pattern was established and applied to expand the "realm of England".

Queen Mary I was the first monarch to begin colonization of Ireland by English settlers.

The Irish people of Kings and Queens County were driven out and their lands given to English colonists. She ascended in 1553.

The O'Briens wrote: "The conquest of Ireland provided the psychological basis, as well as a part of the material basis and training for the colonization of the world". {99 O'Brien p.55} Canny wrote: "Centrally planed and highly structured colonies on classical and militarily lines were first attempted in Ireland in the 1570s..."{100 Canny p.18} It was also considered that force might be needed therein.

Smith wrote: " Ireland, by 1633 had not only been tamed [brutally] by Elizabeth but also colonized by James I, who exported great numbers of Scottish landowners and settlers to Ulster. An Irish-Catholic and landless peasantry was ruled by English-Scottish Protestant overlords." Wentworth the King's Lord Deputy in Ireland had "assiduously promoted colonization in Ireland in 1633...Of all the colonies, Ireland received the greatest number of immigrants throughout the 17th century"{101 Smith p.218}

England gained colonizing experience in Ireland but would soon move with its' European competitors to the western hemisphere. In the middle of the 16th century, English, French, Portuguese ,and Spanish fishermen all used the large island of New Foundland for docking and drying of fish.{102 Quinn p.357} In 1583, Sir Humphrey Gilbert took formal possession of New Foundland for England; more likely, he pretended authority and the Crown pretended it could give it. In 1610, a colony set there became St. Johns.

"At about the time James I succeeded to the throne [1603] and the Spanish war ended ... a new awareness of the role of commerce in society surfaced and overseas colonization benefited from it.

Colonization became identified with the general effort to build up English trade hence attracting widespread public support but also the financial backing of merchants."{103 Shammas p.174}

The 1585 attempt at colonization by the English at Roanoke Island had failed, but in 1607 Virginia was successfully colonized at Jamestown, although it's disheartened colonists were actually sailing away from Jamestown in 1610 when ships coming in from England with supplies and more colonists met them and insisted they return.

"In South America...before the founding of Virginia, Charles Leigh planted a small [English] colony... in Guiana...[but it] miscarried..." {104 Beer "Origin"p.13}

"Sir Thomas Roe...established a small [English] settlement near the river... [Amazon]" {105 Ibid}Probably in the first decade of the 17th century.

The Plymouth Company sent two vessels to the coast of Maine touching a place known as Pemaquid arriving there in early Aug. 1607. "Soon they set for the river [the Kennebec]..." They began a settlement on the river and called it Fort St. George; it was abandoned by the autumn of 1608. {106 Quinn p.407}

In 1609 an English ship headed for Virginia shipwrecked on the island of Bermuda and the ship's party remained there until they could construct two pinnaces from the wreckage. With these they sailed to Jamestown. The pinnaces were next used for an attempted evacuation of Jamestown to New Foundland. The pinnaces were met on their way to New Foundland by the relief ships coming from England and were turned back by them.

"After 1613, it was finally accepted [in England] that no more money should be spent on the search for a northwest passage to Asia, and after that, investors turned their plans further south along the American coast."{107 Quinn p.357}

Capt. Roger North in 1619 set an English settlement on the Amazon, although his charter had been withdrawn. He was imprisoned in England as he had caused a breach with Spain, England apparently had agreed not to settle there. The settlers, however refused to give up the area to Spain. {108 Beer "Origin"p.14}

In Nov./Dec. 1620 the Pilgrims arrived at a place already called Plymouth, (Patuxet was the name of the abandoned Wampanoag Indian village at that site) where they made their permanent settlement. This plantation and its' story has been selected by historians as the ideal to represent the founding of the American settlement, and so it continues.

Roger Williams described how whole Indian villages were abandoned, apparently in the Narragansett country, when a plague called "Wesauashauonck" struck. He wrote that the afflicted were left behind by the survivors. {109 Williams p.210} Such village abandonment may have occurred at Patuxet.

Of the four or five hundred individuals of a particular religious sect referred to as "Separatists", (because they had separated from the Church of England) mentioned as living in England around 1608 , about one hundred and twenty-five were driven out of England in that year. {110Bradford p.19} They found refuge in Netherlands where the freedom of conscience that they wanted was allowed. They were not all satisfied in this foreign country and those dissatisfied sent agents to England to negotiate with moneyed men called adventures for the means to sail and settle in the new world. When some of them finally sailed to America, only forty or more of the hundred passengers were separatists. {111 Bradford p.15}

In 1621, King James I granted to Sir William Alexander the right to establish Nova Scotia (Latin for New Scotland). Later, Scotch settlers immigrated there, although the French had settled there first in 1605.

In 1623, New Hampshire began with the settlement of "Little Harbor."

In 1624, English colonization of Saint Christopher began. {112 Beer"Origin"p.12}

In 1625, the first permanent settlement in Maine occurred at Pemaquid.

In 1627, Barbados and the chief of the islands of the Windward and Leeward were granted to the Earl of Carlisle. There were English there in 1620-1624.

Islands and pieces of the earth were simply granted to members of royalty or those of other power by the King as if they were his to give away and for which he probably received some return favor.

In 1628, Tobago and Trinidad were granted to the Earl of Montgomery. Nevis, Antiqua, Montserrat were all colonized between 1628 and 1633. {113 Beer "Origin"p.12}

In 1628, Massachusetts Bay Colony began with the settlement of colonists from England at a place called Naumkeak, later called Salem. There were already some fishermen dwelling there at times convenient to fishing. {114 Young F.P. p.13&14}

In 1633, the Carolinas came into being as colonies through English grants.

In Mar. 1634, Maryland was colonized directly from England. Two hundred colonists led by Leonard Calvert, planned to found a colony free of religious persecution.

Also in 1634, some Puritans from Massachusetts Bay, led by Thomas Hooker, settled on the Connecticut River at a place they called Wethersfield, beginning Connecticut colony and trouble for the Pequots.

In 1636, Roger Williams and a few others were forced out of land (kindly granted to them by the Wampanoag sachem, Massasoit) by the pretended owners, Plymouth colony. When Williams crossed the river in "mid June 1636" into Narragansett territory, he was granted a spot by the Narragansetts. {115 Knowles p.104} This was the founding of Rhode Island.

Roger Williams is considered by most historians as an early and great champion of democracy and religious freedom, which he was, and as a friend and supporter of the Indians, which he wasn't. He did not seek such distinctions, however, and may have had more interaction with the Indians than any other New Englander of those times. He did many small favors for Indians and was generally in favor with the Narragansetts, but he always watched for the interests of his fellow Englishmen before the needs of the Indians. When troubles were occurring between the Pequots, (who dwelt west of the Narragansetts) and the Puritan colonies in 1636, Gov. Winthrop Sr. of Mass. Bay asked Williams to work against any possible Pequot-Narragansett alliance. Jennings wrote, "He commissioned the exile [Williams had been under orders to be deported back to England who then fled to sachem Massasoit to avoid deportation] to break up the Pequot-Narragansett reconciliation and Williams succeeded just in time." {116 Jennings p.213} The two tribes had been reported as unfriendly. Williams had rushed to the Narragansett chiefs and apparently convinced them not only not to join with the Pequots but to help the English, and indeed he claimed he achieved just that. The Puritan writers give him little or no credit for that service.{117 Bartlet p.333-351} The help the Narragansetts rendered at that time was probably the biggest mistake made by New England natives in that fatal first century; it would have been wise to at least just abstain from the Puritan attack. Helping the English was not a good thing for the Narragansetts for it only increased intertribal animosity. Earlier Williams had written in a letter to the governor of Mass. Bay in 1636 supporting of a plan to have Narragansetts attack some Pequots who had gone to Plum Island fishing, noting "... it will weaken the enemy and distress them , being put by their hopes: as also much enrage the Pequots for ever against them, a thing much desirable."{118 Bartlet p.25} When the Narragansett/Shawomet sachem Punham resisted English acquisitions in their ancestral lands, Williams used his influence upon the supreme sachem, Miantonomi to undermine Pumham. Williams thought the Shawomets could and should pick up and move elsewhere.

When Plymouth's suspicions about Philip heightened in 1675, Williams hastened to the Narragansett chiefs trying to convince them not to side with Philip, assuring them (perhaps feigning their best interests) that they would have no chance of winning against the English who could even get the help of the English King. When he was questioned by those Narragansetts as to why Plymouth could not deal with Philip without the help of the other colonies, he boasted (or claimed he said) that all Englishmen stick together, precisely what he tried to prevent among the Indians. {119 Bartlet p.366-370}

In 1638, a group of Puritans sailed from Mass. Bay to a place opposite Long Island at the mouth of the Quinnipiac River and settled a town latter called New Haven and formed a colony by that same name.

In about 1648, some dwellers at Bermuda sailed to the Bahamas, beginning the first permanent European settlement there. In 1655, Jamaica was captured from Spain by a navel force from England and formally transferred to England in1670.

"In South America English colonial enterprise was represented by Surinam..." {120 Beer "Origins"p.53}

In 1664, an English expedition, led by Colonel Richard Nicolls was directed to conquer the Dutch colony of New Netherlands. The Dutch governor surrendered the colony which then became the colonies of New York and New Jersey.

The above long litany of English colonial expansion occurring in Ireland and the western hemisphere through 1664 is intended to show its extent. Much more continued after 1664 but this much of the movement with its social effects existed in 1675.

I would submit a speculation that the social effect of the colonizing movement was the development of a general attitude in the thought of many English that they had a right to expect to acquire a means of livelihood in some other part of the world, solely because they were English and that important Englishmen had somehow the right to be granted possession of foreign places. These attitudes existed even though it was understood that other humans were long dwelling in those places. Not only were they aware of that, but also that the dwellers there might well oppose them when they attempted to live there. Why, for instance, would the Mayflower passengers spend their nights on board the ship while secure buildings were being built at their chosen spot, Plymouth? Why were garrisons built in all the outlying towns in Mass. Bay until 1676? Rowlandson's Lancaster had five garrisons.

One Mr. Dermer employed by the English adventurer Ferdinando Gorges "for discovery" saw much of the coast of Massachusetts and wrote in "June 30 Anno 1620" in part: " I would that the first plantation might be here [that location being Plymouth] seated, if it come to the number of [at least] fifty persons, or upward. Otherwise Charlton [this likely would be someplace on the river called the Charles River] because there the savages are less to be feared." Dermer was aware of the terrible waste of the natives due to the plague that had just affected that river area but perhaps had not yet stricken Patuxet. {121 Bradford p.89} It is said that more than fifty of the early colonial villages were built upon the sites of native villages abandoned due to the plague. It was well known to the promoters of colonization that hostility by natives had to be considered as likely, although they down-played that possibility to would- be colonists.

England, Spain, Portugal, France, Netherlands and Sweden all engaged in colonization. The control of some colonies changed from one power to another usually through some form of coercion.

With the clear exception of Bermuda, in all these places where settlements were attempted, native inhabitants were living nearby or having some use of the land at times. In southern New England, as a result of the ravages of recent plagues, there were many acres of land cleared by the natives that looked abandoned or were, at least temporarily abandoned, land that English settlers took to use as their own farmland.

Barbados, that often mentioned mid-sized Caribbean island was without natives at the time of colonization in 1627, but historical and archaeological evidence shows that the island was occupied by natives before that time. The likely cause of depopulation of Barbados was probably due to Spanish slave hunters active in those islands in earlier decades. {122 Handler p.39}

Conveniently to the purposes of exploitation and colonization, the Europeans decided the natives had no real claim to land or, if they might have some sort of claim in anyone's opinion, it could be easily compensated for.

In the English colonization movement, there were almost always moneyed Englishmen who saw the opportunity to acquire more wealth through investing in and promoting exploration and or colonization.

People were needed for colonization, and, in England, there were many poor people willing to chance getting a better life in the new world.. Hill wrote - "The years from 1620 to 1650 [in England] were bad ;the 1640's were much the worst decade of the period."{123 Hill p.86} In addition, there were many new religious sects in England, and their members were often being persecuted by the government and the Church of England. Some of those who sought freedom of religion were willing to move when solicited to do so by the promoters of colonies. The government in England itself saw an advantage in colonization. "In the eyes of the English government [cir. 1660] colonial expansion was a subordinate, though vital, part of the larger movement of commercial progress."{124 Beer "Origin" p.18}

Perhaps the Puritans were not a sect but a radical part of the Church of England; however many Puritans (a title they rejected) favored forming their own place to live and to practice their own form of Christianity. Efforts were going on in England to suppress Puritans. Massachusetts Bay was just such a place for them. "It was stated that 21,200 [persons] had arrived in the fifteen years from 1629 to 1643" in Mass. Bay, mostly Puritans.{125 Beer "Origin"p.284} During that period, Puritans were gaining strength in England, and the civil war, championed by the Puritans broke out in 1642. The King, Charles I was captured in that war and on Jan.27th 1649 and was "sentenced to death as Tyrant, Traitor, Murderer, and public enemy...".{126 Cannon p.385} With Puritans in control of Parliament and Oliver Cromwell as Lord Protector, there was a new England for Puritans at home and immigration to Mass. Bay dried up .

Thomas Hutchinson, a Massachusetts governor and later historian wrote of that time- "The motive to transportation [sic] to America was over, by the change in affairs of England- The importation of settlers now ceased."{127 T. Hutchinson p.82} Clearly the freedom to practice their Puritanism was a factor in the amount of immigration into Mass. Bay, but that was not the motive of adventurer/ promoters.

Beer wrote- "Though the religious motive in colonization figured very prominently in the writings of the day -the spread of Christianity is specifically mentioned as one of the objects in view in nearly all the colonial charters...yet it cannot be considered as one of the determining causes of the movement" {128 Beer "Origin" p.29} The hope of self-betterment of the poor English must have also been a factor in their transporting to the colonies, even by Puritans and other persecuted Christians. The laments of ministers over the "slacking off" of their flocks after settlement attest to a motive of self-betterment in many settlers. So it would seem the motives of government, adventurers/promoters, and, at least in part, the settlers were built on self-interest. The lament of the sincere Gov. William Bradford, expressed in a note he wrote sometime after 1650, tells how he the Plymouth governor viewed the attitudes of his colonists at that time; "O sacred bond [amongst the first Pilgrims] whilst invoilably preserved! How sweet and precious were the fruits that flowed from the same! But when this fidelity decayed, then their ruin approached. ...that subtle serpent hath slyly wound in himself under fair pretences of necessity and the like, to untwist these sacred bonds..." {128b Bradford p.34} I submit it was the seeking of each colonist's self interest that caused what Bradford saw as that "decay".

The real needs of natives were dismissed with the help of often pretended reasons other than self interest. The colonization, propelled by whatever the stated motives were, brought immense harm to the natives of the lands colonized. That was bad enough, but the perceived need for and the implementation of slavery in some of the colonies compounded the evil.

Chapter Sixteen

✦

Slavery

Slavery was practiced far back in historic times by larger or more powerful societies than neighboring societies upon members of the neighboring societies. It usually occurred when a society developed powerful central control and conceived of the value of slave labor.

The Portuguese were the first European nation to begin the importation of slaves beginning in 1444. These were Africans captured from western Africa. Spain soon followed with slavery in tropical Latin America. During the 16th century, Spanish colonists forced natives to work the land in their new colonies, but they died off too easily, and the importation of Negroes became the preferred enslavement policy. England entered the slave trade in the late 16th century to supply the Spanish colonies.

Some religious men did condemn the mistreatment of the natives. In 1537, Pope Paul III did proclaim something against Indian slavery; "Indians themselves indeed are true men" and should not be "deprived of their liberty" and "reduced to our service like brute animals".

The Spanish missionary Bartolome de Las Casas (1474-1566) was most vocal in his opposition.

Las Casas castigated all those who supported the Spanish activities in the New World; "All this drags innumerable souls to ruin and blocks the service of spreading the Christian religion by closing the eyes of those who, crazed by blind ambition, bend all their energies of mind and body to the one purpose of gaining wealth, power, honors and dignities. For the sake of these things they kill and destroy with inhuman cruelty people who are completely innocent, meek, harmless, temperate, and quite ready...to receive and embrace the word of God". {129 Las Casas p.

26}; "He who wants a large part of mankind to be such that, following Aristotle's teaching [who provided a justification of slavery], he may act like a ferocious executioner toward them, press them into slavery and through them grow rich, is a despotic master, not a Christian; a son of Satan, not of God; a plunderer, not a shepherd ; a person who is by the spirit of the devil, not heaven."{130 Las Casas p.40}

Las Casas wrote much more than this; he was a thorn in the side of Spanish adventurers. Spain claimed to be a very Christian kingdom so missionaries who talked like Las Casas presented problems; however, Spain continued in notorious activities, as did the English Christians.

In North America, the first Negro slaves were landed at Jamestown in 1619.

In 1637 after the English victory in the Pequot War, hundreds of Pequots were enslaved by the English, and others were given to their allies, the Mohegans and the Narragansetts. Over time those given to allies seemed to regain their independence. Conn. governor John Winthrop Jr. also helped some Pequots establish their own separate village.

In 1652, Maryland planned an expedition against the Indians in which - "the captive Indians were to be sold". {131 Lauber p.205}

Beer wrote; "In 1655, or there abouts, the planters [of Barbados] stated that Barbados...had 20,000 Negroes..."{132Beer "Origins" p.413}

Lauber wrote; "The Indians of Rhode Island gave much trouble by stealing the goods and cattle of the colonist. To prevent it, a law passed in 1659, to the effect that, if the damage exceeded twenty shillings, the convict might be sold as a slave to any English plantation abroad unless he made restitution."{133 Lauber p.205}

Beer wrote, "Towards the end of 1660, the first African Company of the restoration was formed..."solely for the slave trade.{134 Beer "Old Col."p.325} Since that company was not strong enough to compete with the Dutch in that trade, a new company, "Royal Adventures", was chartered with strong backing of Englishmen including Charles II, which should remove any doubt about slavery being accepted by that king. Before 1660, England's government did not directly support African slave capture and trade from the African coast, although it was carried on by the English as a private venture before that time.

By about 1668 several estimates of the Negro slave population on Barbados, ranged from 40,000 to 80,000{134b Ibid p.320} In 1668 prices for Negro slaves were quoted at 12 to 16 pounds per head and later 25 pounds per head.{135 Ibid p.337}

In the southern colonies, Lauber wrote, "In Sept. 1671 war was declared against the Kussoe [tribe] ... the Kussoe were quickly defeated and the prisoners were sent to be sold out of the colony." {136 Lauber p.119}

Beer quoted Ferdinando Gorges who, in addition to his inherited right to Maine, had important interests in the West Indies. Gorges wrote, in 1674, "that only colonies of the plantation type should be encouraged". Beer also quoted a number of Englishmen who expressed the opinion that only the slave/plantation types of colonies were helpful to the mother county. The northern continental colonies produced the same products as England, especially New England, and, therefore, were not approved. {137 Beer "Old Colonial"p.47} Plantations, (which used slaves) which produced goods needed in England were approved of thereby.

"During the Indian wars in Virginia [cir. 1675], Gov. Berkeley ... in a letter to Robert Smith, military commander in the Rappahanock country, not only proposed that a war of extinction be waged against the northern Indians , but also suggested that the colonial government defray the expenses of the undertaking by disposal of the Indian women and children [as slaves]."{138 Lauber p.131}

"During Bacon's rebellion in 1676, the [Virginian] assembly at his instigation declared the enslavement of Indians for life to be legal, and made provisions for granting Indians to soldiers as a partial inducement to volunteer."{139 Ibid p.131}

The despicable enslavement behavior of the southern colonies shows that the distorted morality of the New England Puritans regarding enslavement was no worse than that of some of the southern colonial leaders.

A small number of individual Indians had been sold out of New England in the decades before King Philip's War, but once the war began, Plymouth sold groups of Wampanoags out of the country as early as July or August of 1675. After July of the next year, large numbers of surrendering or captured Indians were sold out of the country.

Some of the older colonial soldiers, probably officers, had served in the civil war in England and in the following conquest of Ireland. In Ireland, they had seen the Irish natives pursued and captured and knew that many of those were sent into slavery, so the same procedure with the Indians may have been seen by them as normal.

"Between June 25 and Sept.26, 1676 alone, the Mass. Bay colony received 397.13 pounds for 188 prisoners of war sold..." {140 Lepore p.154}

In Barbados, the Assembly, in fear of having too many violent Indian captives as slaves on their island, passed an act in June 1676 addressing that concern. The explanation of the act provided by the Assembly had these words "...to prevent the bringing of Indian slaves, and as well to send away and transport those already brought to this island from New England and the adjacent colonies, being thought a people of too subtle, bloody and dangerous inclination to be and remain here..." {141 Handler p.57} Jamaica had also passed a similar law.

After the war there was considerable debate among the ministers whether it was correct to execute Philip's son for the "sins" of his father or to sell him out of the country. Finally, both he and his mother were sold out of the country.

Records of the Royal African Company give the total number of Negroes delivered to Jamaica from 1680 to 1688 as 18,802 souls, In addition, privateers also brought in an untold number, but Beer thinks the Company probably delivered four times more than the privateers.

These bits of history concerning the development of slavery in the new world up to cir. 1676 give some idea of how widely this evil was grasped upon and how it was used in conjunction with the conquest or usurpation of land from natives.

It seems to be an ability in human nature to be able to degrade in one's own mentality another social group or ethnic people or even an individual. With possession of such a mentality, it is allowable to dispossess, abuse or use the degraded person or people. Prejudice and bias are agents of such degrading.

From here let us return to the question- Why didn't any of early colonial writers of New England see that the colonists were all in a process of usurping the land of the natives? The simple answer, again, is they did not want to, and their mentality was assisted therein by their absorption of distorted religious interpretations as well as the experience of the injustices and inequalities of their own royal English traditions.

Chapter Seventeen

✦

Pretense Assailed

Not all Englishmen shared that mentality. In the work, " The World Turned Upside Down" by Christopher Hill, it would appear certain, that there was plenty of opposition in England to royalty, to the wealthy, to the established church, to the private holding of land, to much religious teaching, to lawyers and to much of traditional morality. Hill wrote- "Even Oliver Cromwell [the Protector] as late as 1650, said 'the law as it is now constituted serves only to maintain the lawyers and to encourage the rich to oppress the poor.' " {142 Hill p.217} "...some radicals denied the civilizing mission of white Anglo- Saxon protestants" {Ibid p.271} Also, Hill wrote, "Already in 1646, Thomas Edwards reported seditious spirits who were questioning Englishmen's rights in Ireland. Walwyn suggested they had no business to be there at all, 'the cause of the Irish natives in seeking their just freedoms...was the very same as our cause here [the Civil War] in endeavoring our own rescue and freedom from the power of oppressor's.' " {143 Hill p.271}

While the Puritans of New England did have many sympathizers and friends in old England they seemed to have had many opponents in old England who strongly disliked their behavior in the New World. That enmity was especially expressed towards Mass. Bay, and there was a willingness to blame Mass. Bay for the war of 1675.

That could be typical anti-Mass. Bay feelings, but Gerrard Winstanley went much further in his criticism of the English government itself. Winstanley was a prominent Englishman who was bankrupt by the Civil War and nearly persecuted under the Commonwealth.{144 Hill p8} Winstanley wrote- "Not one word was spoken [by God] in the beginning that one branch of mankind should rule over another...

But... selfish imaginations...did set up one man to teach and rule over another. And that the earth that is within this creation made a common storehouse for all, is bought and sold and kept in the hands of a few, whereby the great Creator is mightily dishonored, as if he were a respecter of persons, delighting in the comfortable livelihood of some and rejoicing in the poverty and straits of others."{145 Hill p.106 or Orwell p.121&122}. In 1649 Winstanley wrote THE TRUE LEVELERS....

Two words, tyrant and hypocrite were combined in the title of a pamphlet published in 1649 in Rotterdam, entitled "Tyranipocrit Discovered". The editors of BRITISH PAMPHLETEERS wherein "T.D." appears, write of it; "There appears to be no clue to the authorship of this remarkable pamphlet perhaps the best of all revolutionary works during the Protectorate and Commonwealth- The author was evidently one of the radicals who incurred the displeasure of Cromwell....and had taken refuge abroad..."{146 Orwell p.81}

Hill wrote that T.D.'s author in one part, "attacked the government of the English Commonwealth for not having established 'an equality of goods and lands' as God and nature would have it... 'the rich thieves [who] make a combination and call it the law, to hang a poor man if he do steal, when they have wrongfully taken from him all his maintenance.'" T.D. continued, "They make themselves thieves by Act of parliament... ." T.D. suggests what should have been done after overthrowing the king was- "To give unto every man with discretion so near as may be an equal share of earthly goods."{147 Hill p.93 or Orwell p. 96,103,108}

Hill wrote; "The author of T.D. Made some gentler points against the selfishness and hypocrisy to which Puritanism could give rise- 'I would not dispraise faith, but I would praise love, and prefer love above and before all...Man may profit man, but no man can profit God; and therefore, if [we] will do good we must do it to mankind, and not to God without [i.e. outside] man... Faith no doubt is a comfortable thing for him that hath it, but another's faith cannot help me.'" {147 Hill p.270 or Orwell p. 86&89}

T.D. also includes thought on England's world-wide activities, words of truth that could be seen by any who cared to accept them. "Our merchants they travel by sea and land to make Christian proselytes, chiefly [that is] our Indian merchants; but consider their practices, and the profit we have by their double dealing, first in robbing the poor Indians of that which God had given them, and then bringing it home to us, that we may thereby the better set forth and show the pride of our hearts in decking our proud carcasses, and feeding our greedy guts with superfluous unnecessary curiosities."

Further "although their dealing concerning the Indians goods be bad, yet they deal worser with their persons, for they either kill them, which is bad, or make them slaves which is worse."{148 Hill p.271 Orwell p. 90}

Chapter Eighteen

✦

Indian Hospitality

Returning to Mary, where by Quanapin's guidance, she visited her son Joesph, somewhere in the Ashuelot valley in New Hampshire. "When I came to him I found him not well...he had a boyl on his side which much troubled him: We bemoaned one another awhile, as the Lord helped us, and then I returned again." After returning, Mary, undoubtedly starving, began "going among the Wigwams, I went into one, and there found a Squaw who showed herself very kind to me, and gave me a piece of Bear. I put it into my pocket and came home, but could not find an opportunity to boil it for fear they would get it from me... In the morning I went to the same Squaw, who had a Kettle of Ground-Nuts boiling; I asked her to let me boyle my piece of Bear in her Kettle, which she did, and gave me some Ground -nuts to eat with it : and I cannot but think how pleasant it was to me.

"One bitter cold day, I could find no room to sit down before the fire: [in her captor's wigwam]...but I went into another Wigwam, where they were also sitting round the fire, but the Squaw laid a skin for me, and bid me sit down, and gave me some Ground-Nuts, and bade me come again...and yet they were strangers to me that I never saw before." They said they would "buy" her if they could.

On the day of the tenth removal, "part of the Company removed about three quarters of a mile"... and set their wigwams. "being hungry I went again to the place we were before at, to get something to eat: being encouraged by the Squaw's kindness... when I was there, there came an Indian to look after me, who when he found me, kickt me all along." It appears Quanapin's party was annoyed at Mary's begging and probably embarrassed by it. The kicking of Mary was one of two instances of physical abuse during her captivity. Mary was certainly naïve in her expectations of what her captors might tolerate. " I went home and found Venison roasting that night, but they would not give me one bit of it Sometimes I met with favor, and sometimes with nothing but frowns." Mary should be considered fortunate when and if she only received frowns in response to some of her actions. Her narrative makes her seem more brazen than timid.

The favor she met with is in accord with the Rev. Heckewelder's description of hospitality and sharing by those Indians with whom he lived in close association for sixteen years. John Heckewelder was born in1743 in Bedford, England. His father was a native of Moravia who moved first to Germany and then to England helping to establish his particular Christian movement there before going to Bethlehem, Pa. with his eleven- year- old son, John. John became a full-time missionary in 1771 in Pennsylvania to Indian converts who were called Moravian Indians. All the original converts were of the Monsey tribe (considered as Lenni-Lenape or so-called Delawares); more Lenni-Lanape and Mahicans were later added. They were all of the Algonquin language speaking people, as were all of the New England tribes. {149 Heckewelder p.VIII& Intro.}

In his "History, Manners & Customs of the Indians..." Heckewelder wrote, "they are never in search of excuses to avoid giving, but freely supply their neighbor's wants from the stock prepared for their own use. They give and are hospitable to all, without exception, and will always share with each other and often with the stranger, even to their last morsel. They would rather lie down themselves on a empty stomach, than have it laid to their charge that they had neglected their duty, by not satisfying the wants of a stranger, the sick or the needy." {150 Heckewelder p.171}

Roger Williams says virtually the same of his benefactors, the Narragansetts, in his "Key to the Language" written when he sailed to England in 1643. Therein he wrote; "...they are remarkably free and courteous, to invite all Strangers in: and if any come to them upon any occasion, they request them to come in, if they not come in of themselves... . I have acknowledged among them an heart sensible of kindness, and have reaped kindness again from many, seaven years after, when I myself had forgotten..." {151 Williams p.97} Shamefully, however his later writings refer to the Indians contemptuously.

Williams, when fleeing from expulsion from Mass. Bay, sought help from the Wampannoag sachem Massasoit who allowed him a spot in their domain to settle and farm. When the reverends of Mass. Bay heard of this, they complained of it to the authorities of Plymouth, as in their mentality, the whole Wampanoag domain was Plymouth's and Williams should not be tolerated. Plymouth informed Williams that he must leave that location . Williams, a respecter of Plymouth's pretended ownership moved to the domain of the Narragansetts where sachem Miantonomi granted him a spot. Despite receiving such hospitality and despite having even been saved from drowning in Narragansett Bay by Indians, he continually disparaged Indians, in his letters, with such words as "filthy savages", "barbarians" and "barbarous scum".

Williams was a Puritan before he fled Mass. Bay, but he would soon reject all organized religions awaiting future prophets who would guide men correctly. Hill wrote; "...a rejection of all sects, of all organized worship- Such men were called Seekers- Walwyn...Roger Williams, John Saltmarsh, John Milton, probably Oliver Cromwell himself" were such.{152 Hill p.144 }

Daniel Gookin, writing of the "Praying Indians" under his supervision wrote; "They are much given to hospitality in their way. If any strangers come to their houses, they will give to him the best lodging and diet they have; and the strangers must be first be served, by themselves."{153 Gookin "Hist. Coll." p13}

Chapter Ninteen

✦

Fauna and Flora

The eleventh removal was said to be the furthest north Mary was taken and that was somewhere near present-day Pisgah State Park, New Hampshire.

Neil Jorgensen wrote; "In 1927 Harvard Univ. was given twenty acres of virgin timber on Mt. Pisgah ..." . That was all that was then left of New England's primeval hardwood forest but that too was almost totally destroyed by the unusual passage of the hurricane of 1938. There were a few much smaller tracts still left standing. Some of the hemlocks destroyed were found to be 400 years old, and would have been alive when Mary was there. If Mary's party did not pass through any of those twenty acres, they certainly passed through many acres of similar primeval forests.

It was not just the native people that suffered so badly from the European invasion, as this also degraded the fauna and flora. Many species of animals have been driven out New England or have retreated to remote corners. Not all of New England was covered by the fully mature primeval forests in 1676, but it was almost all covered by forests. Some of the early explorers noted that the forests crowded right up to the shores. Even the islands were forested shore to shore. Natives in the south did clear many acres for their fields and settlements, many of which the English used when they found them vacant (vacant either because of the great loss of natives due to the plague or intentionally left idle to naturally re-fertilize) but that clearing was little compared to the clearing after 1676.

Jorgensen wrote; "In the middle of the 19th century... a completely deforested southern New England ...did seem a possibility. At this time, somewhere between 75 & 85% of the regions southern half was already field and pasture... . Most of present-day southern New England forests have grown within the span of human memory... . Young woodlands often bear little resemblance to the mature forests that once stood in their stead. Usually an entirely different community of trees will appear in woodlands that have been logged, cleared or burned; often centuries will pass before the forest will once more return to it's original state."{154 Jorgensen p.142}

Anyone who loves nature and has had the experience of passing through a primeval forest will recognize the beauty and magnificence of such a forest. Magnificence, in this case, can be said to be only in the eye of the beholder, that is it can't be qualified, but it may be quantified by the attainment of the great growth of trees therein. Jorgensen wrote; "In comparison to the present-day northern hardwood forests the estimated volume of timber on this virgin [Pisgah] tract was fantastic. About 33,000 board- feet per acre was the average of the whole twenty acre tract, about ten times as much as the estimated average volume of today's northern woodlands. Thirty-three thousand board-feet was only the average, on some tracts the volume was much higher up to an incredible 85,000 board-feet."{155 Jorgensen p.188} All of this, of course, made little or no impression on English colonists, certainly not on a captive.

One of the rationalizations used to justify the usurping of land by the English, notably by Mass. Bay's most famous leader Winthrop, was that the English "improved" the land by clearing it. The natives had done little clearing and, therefore, had little entitlement. From a ecological view point, those lands were certainly not "improved" by clearing.

Chapter Twenty

✦

Nutrition, Health and Disease

On the day of her 12th, removal Mary recorded; "My mistress [Weetamoe]...was gone to the burial of a Papoos, and returning she found me sitting and reading in my Bible; she snatched it... and threw it out the doors; I ran out and catch it up, and put it in my pocket, and never let her see it afterward. Then they packed up their things... and gave me my load. I complained it was too heavy whereupon she gave me a slap in the face [the second physical abuse], and bade me go... their insolency grew worse and worse."

Weetamoe seemed to really dislike Mary. She was the sachem of the Pocasset/Wampanoag; she had succeeded her deceased father Corbitant. Her sister Wootonekanuske was the wife of Philip. Her first husband was Wamsutta, alias Alexander, Philip's older brother. As mentioned earlier, Weetamoe had left Philip's party after the battle at Nipsachuck and gone to the Narragansetts later becoming Quanapin's wife, her third husband. Apparently she had left her second husband called Peter.

The 12th remove occurred on Sunday April, 9th. That day Mary notes; "This morning I asked my Master whither he would sell me to my Husband; he answered me Nux, [yes] which did much rejoyce my spirit." From there on, their track led back towards Mt. Wachusetts, with a slight reverse that very day, "... for when we had gone a little way, on a sudden my mistress gives out, she would go no further... and she called her Sannup, [husband] and would have him go back also [north in present-day New Hampshire?], but he would not, but said, He would go on, and come to us in three days." The whole Indian party was heading back to warring, and it seems Weetamoe wanted no part of it. "My master being gone, who seemed to me the best friend that I had of an Indian, both in cold and hunger, and quickly so it proved." What made Quanapin her "best friend" and how it proved quickly is not specified unless it was his decision to agree to her redemption, but that did not occur until May, 2nd which doesn't seem to suit "quickly". Perhaps there was another unrecorded kindness.

That evening "going out... and walking among the Trees, I found six Acorns and two Chestnuts, which were some refreshment to me. Towards Night I gathered me some sticks for my own comfort, but when I came to ly down they bade me to go out, and ly somewhere-else, for they had company come in more than their own: [with the company their wigwam could not even hold all the regulars?] I told them, I could not tell where to go, they bade me go look; I told them, if I went to another Wigwam they would be angry, and send me home again. Then one of the Company drew his sword and told me he would run me through if I did not go presently. Then was I fain to stoop to this fellow... I went to one Wigwam, and they told me they had no room. Then I went to another, and they said the same; at last an old Indian bade me to come to him, and his Squaw gave me some Ground-nuts; she gave me also something to lay under my head, and a good fire we had: and through the good providence of God, I had a comfortable lodging that night, In the morning another Indian bade me come at night, and he would give me six Ground-nuts, which I did."

The mixed response of the Indians on this occasion, while not as laudable as the descriptions of Heckewelder, Gookin or Williams, it should be considered that the status of Mary was that of a captive, and she "belonged" to a certain wigwam, not to others. Also the status of the parties approached was not the same as Indians seated in their home village. Those she approached were under the pressure of food shortage and the need to regularly pick-up and move considerable distances. Even under these circumstances, she found some who took her in and fed her.

It has often been written that the Indians, at certain times of the year, lived in semi-starvation and that may be a true statement for some parts of the New World, but it appears to be untrue for the Indians of southern New England.

Howard Russel wrote; "all in all, from wood, waters and his cultivated fields, the New England Indian usually ate well and with greater variety than did many North American tribes. His ordinary food contained all essential calories, vitamins, minerals, acid and trace elements necessary for healthy enduring bodies and active ingenious minds. Yet when forced by circumstances- such as the necessity for swift removal- to go without food, Indians could stoically endure fasting."{156 Russel p.93} Russel mentioned 11 vegetables, 23 fruits, 16 fish, 5 shell-fish, all types of animals (usually excluding pure carnivores) that were eaten by New England Indians and there were undoubtedly other items. Snails were eaten and possibly some insects.

Charles Man wrote; "According to one modern reconstruction, Downland [east-coast Indian] diets at the time [1600] averaged about 2500 calories a day, a higher level than those in famine-racked Europe."{157 Man "Smithsonian" Dec. 2005 p. 98}

Russel quoted Alvin M. Joseph from "The Indian Heritage of America"- "Today [1980] four-sevenths of the agricultural production of the United States measured in farm values, consists of economic plants domesticated by the Indian and taken over by the white man."{158 Russel p.6} It is believed much of this domestication originated in prehistoric central and South America.

As to some specifics of the New England Indian diet, Russell wrote; "The most common ground maize dish, the true staff of life was 'samp' or 'newsamp', a kind of porridge, which Roger Williams says 'is the wholesome diet they have'.{159 Russell p.76}... Almost as valuable as maize to the aboriginal cook were beans. At their tender stage the two were 'seethed' together to form 'sutsquthahhash'. Dietitians find both corn and beans, excellent sources of protein; and beans, which contain albumin and amino acids, in both of which maize is deficient, supplement it by adding nutritional value." {160 Russell p.79}..."The Indian methods of preparing and combining food...have been of considerable variety, they resulted in a diet diversified and balanced, contributing to a lithe and healthy body, vigorous and with stamina."{161 Russell p.92} This general good health, vigor and spirit of the young Indian was in marked contrast to the misery of many children reported of in Europe in the 16th and 17th centuries.

Giovanni da Verrazano, sailing north along the present coast of the United States in1523, noted that it was "densely populated". It is believed that he anchored in Narragansett Bay where an Indian came aboard, a tall, long- haired man "as beautiful of stature and build as I can possibly describe."{162 Beer "Origins p.100 }

The Reverend Francis Higginson, sailing to Salem aboard the "Talbot" and arriving on June 29, 1629, kept an extensive journal of the trip and some of his first encounters on shore, in it he wrote of the natives; "For their statures they are strong limbed people."{163 Higginson p.256}

John Josselyn sailed to New England in 1638 and, as a nascent-scientist, he set about writing of and listing all of his observations while in New England. He reported of the natives: "As for their persons they are tall and handsome people...". {164 Josselyn "Two Voyages" p.89} And from his other work -"...the Women many of them have very good Features...even short Teeth and very white... handsome streight Bodies...Their limbs cleanly streight, and of convenient stature..." {165 Josselyn"N.E. Rarities" p.99}

Gookin on the same subject said "...the proportion of their limbs well formed; it is rare to see a crocked person among them."{166 Gookin" Hist. Coll." p.4}

William Wood came to New England in 1629 and returned to England in 1633, He wrote a long promotional tract about the settlements with a great deal of information seemingly directed at future settlers. He wrote of the "Northward" New England Indians (he was based in Boston) ; "First of their stature, most of them being between five or six foot high, straight bodies, strongly composed, smooth skinned, merry countenance ...broad shouldered, brawny armed, long and slender handed...small wasted, lank bellied, well thighed, flat kneed, handsome grown legs, and small feet.... have been in many places, yet did I never see one that was born either in redundance or defect a monster, or any that sickness had deformed, or casualty made decrepit..."{167 W. Wood p.82}

From the contemporary description of the physical appearance of the New England Indians and the present-day appreciation of the high value of the Indian diet of those times, we should conclude that most of those Indians lived healthy lives.

This was not at all the situation after the plagues arrived early in the 17th century, undoubtedly from contact with Europeans. These plagues swept though Indian villages on and off for many decades with varying degrees of severity.

Some of the deformities in English children were caused by old world diseases and not necessarily by poor diet or poor life-style. The old world diseases that led to the plagues had a terrible effect on native Americans, and good life-style and good diet probably gave little or no advantage against them. In New England, the first plague that struck is said to have occurred in 1616 and that in the coastal villages. Another major plague was noted in 1633-1635.

The English, known as the "Pilgrims", in 1620, settled at the vacated village site of Patuxet, vacated by a plague. In July of 1621, Edward Winslow and Steven Hopkins were sent by that settlement, called Plymouth, to visit Massasoit, the so-called supreme sachem of the Wamanoags. They were guided by a survivor of Patuxet called Squanto. From William Bradford's account; "They found the place to be 40 miles from hence, the soil good and the people not many, being dead and abundantly wasted in the late great mortality, which fell in all these parts about three years before the coming of the English [both English and French ships had frequented the shores and made contact with the natives before 1620] wherein thousands of them had died. They not being able to bury one another, their sculls and bones were found in many places lying still above the ground...a very sad spectacle to behold. ...But... the Narragansetts living but on the other side of that great bay...had not been not at all touched with the wasting plague."{168 Bradford p.96-97}

John Winthrop Sr., who was called the leader of the "Great Migration" and often Mass. Bay's governor, said the plague was due to Smallpox. Many thought the wasting of the natives was a favor from God for the benefit of the colonists. The concept of contagion was widely understood and the word regularly used by the English at that time. However, any understanding of relative immunity was not even hinted at in colonial writings of that period. The Europeans had acquired some immunity to certain diseases but carried such diseases to people who had little or no immunity to them. Cotton Mather in 1721 actually championed inoculations against smallpox, which suggests an understanding of induced immunity on his part. Both the Pilgrims at their Connecticut

River trading post and the Puritans at Mass. Bay reported their help and charity towards neighboring natives afflicted by the plague.

Alfred Crosby wrote; "Smallpox is a disease that combines virulence and extreme communicability and has no dormant state in humans...it can only rage, it cannot lurk."{169 Crosby p.309}

Jared Diamond wrote; "Imagine smallpox being introduced into a small and isolated population with out any previous exposure to smallpox or related viruses. If all the people have plenty of contact with one another, then smallpox will quickly spread infecting everybody. Many people will die, but those who survive will develop antibodies to smallpox and thereby will become resistant. As a result, smallpox will have killed or immunized the whole population and will die out..." {170 Diamond p.26} It, however, may be reintroduced into those born after the first plague dies out, by newly infected individuals.

Crosby wrote; "It appeared for the first time in Siberia in 1630, crossing the Urals from Russia and passing through the ranks of the [natives]... like a scythe through grain. The death rate in a single epidemic could soar past 50%."{171 Crosby p.38}

Some accounts have stated death rates in New England as high as 90%. Whatever the pathogen was in New England, it seems to have followed a course like those described above.

In King Philip's War, reports have many Indians dying of sickness, but not in numbers as in the earlier plagues. However, the prolonged scarcity of food to those Indians surely affected their physical strength as well as that of their captives. The natives were disposed to accepting going for long periods of time without eating. Even under normal conditions one meal per day was the norm. However, they may have been self-deceived by an expectation that they could endure even in the much longer periods of deprivation such as the war. Even if physically able to keep going, perhaps their mental facilities such as willpower, judgment, patience and dreams may have been negatively affected. Dreams were often taken as directives from other-world spirits. Since the warring natives made a number of bad decisions in the second half of 1676, it is possible that nutritional shortage played a part in those decisions.

Chapter Twenty One

✦

Quanapin Returns

At the location reached on the 13th removal, near present Hinsdale, New Hampshire Mary noted "Here one asked me to make a shirt for her Papoos, for which she gave me a mess of Broth... and to make it the better, she had put into it about a handful of Pease, and a few roasted Ground nuts."

"I had not seen my son a pritty while, and here was an Indian of whom I made inquiry after him, and asked him when he saw him: he answered me, that such a time his master roasted him, and that he was a very good meat: But the Lord upheld my Spirit, under this discouragement; and I considered their horrible addictedness to lying, and there is not one of them that makes the least conscience of speaking of truth."

Since Mary doesn't mention horror, but "discouragement" at this Indian's story and her noting of their "lying" indicate that she never really believed the Indian's story.

At this same place, Mary also told of an incident happening as she was lying beside the campfire and moving a branch within the fire hoping to have more heat for herself. A squaw there threw some fire ashes at Mary's face and Mary thought she would be blinded but recovered her sight in the morning.

"At about this time they came yelping from Hadly, where they had killed three English men, and brought one Captive with them, viz. Thomas Read. They all gathered about the poor Man, asking him many Questions. I desired also to go and see him; and when I came, he was crying bitterly, supposing they would quickly kill him. Whereupon I asked one of them, whether they intended to kill him; he answered me, they would not: He being a little cheared [Mary believed that Indian apparently] ...I asked him about the wel-fare of my Husband, he told me he saw him such a time in the Bay, and that he was well, but very melancholly... Some of them told me he was dead, and they had killed him some said he was married again, and that the governor wished him to Marry...So like were these barbarous creatures to him [the devil?] who was a lyer from the beginning."

"As I was sitting once in the Wigwam here Philip's Maid came in with the Child in her arms, and asked me to give her a piece of my Apron, to make a flap for it, [Philip's son would be too old to be in the maid's arms. Was the child the maid's?] I told her I would not: then my Mistress bad me give it, but still I said no: the maid told me if I would not give her a piece, she would tear a piece off it: I told her I would tear her coat then, with that my Mistress rises up, and takes up a stick big enough to have killed me, and struck at me with it, but I step out, and she struck the stick into the Mat of the Wigwam. But while she was pulling it out, I ran to the Maid and gave her all of my Apron, and so that storm went over." If Mary had heard of the story of the killing of captive Goodwife Joslin, it is hard to believe the captive Mary would be so insolent as she was here. We also see the impatience of Weetamoe.

At this same place, Mary, hearing that her son was also there, went to see him and informed him that his Father was well "but very melancholly". The son said he was as much grieved for the father as he was for himself. Mary "wondered at his speech, for I thought I had enough upon my spirit in reference to my self, to make me mindless of my Husband and everyone else: they being safe among their Friends." Maybe most people would feel as Mary did, but most would not admit of it. This indicates Mary's frankness and honesty and makes her narrative thereby more valuable. "He told me also, that a while before, his Master [together with other Indians] were going to the French for Powder; but by the way the Mohawks met with them and killed four of their company which made the rest turn back again..."

Also there Mary sought out "an English Youth ...one John Gilberd of Springfield. I found him lying without dores, upon the ground; ...he told me he was sick of a flux, with eating so much blood: They had turned him out of the Wigwam, and with him an Indian Papoos, (whose parents had been killed) almost dead in a bitter cold day... the young man had nothing on, but his shirt and wastcoat. This sight was enough to melt a heart of flint. There they lay quivering in the Cold, the youth round like a dog; the Papoos stretcht out' with his eyes and nose and mouth full of dirt, and yet alive and groaning. I advised John to go and get [to] some fire: he told me he could not stand, but I perswaded him still...with much ado I got him to a fire, and went myself home. As soon as I was got home, his Master's daughter came after me, to know what I had done with the English man…" Mary told her how she had got him to a fire, and then she led her to him. By the time Mary returned to her wigwam, she had been suspected of trying to escape. Those of her wigwam "began to rant and domineer" telling her not to stir again from the wigwam. Here it is obvious from Mary's words that there were Indians who intended to keep Gilberd, but the lack of care of the papoose is unaccountable or callous.

Mary was, thereafter, imprisoned in the wigwam with nothing to eat until the next day when an Indian came to the wigwam asking if Mary would reknit an overlarge pair of stockings he wished to use. Mary had him "ask my mistress if I might go with him a little way; she said yes, I might…" After Mary did the repair, "...he gave me some roasted Ground-nuts…"

Mary's son soon after came again to visit her. "He told me...that he was very hungry..." Mary "...bid him to go into the Wigwams as he went along... Which he did, and it seems tarried a little too long; for his Master was angry with him, and beat him, and then sold him. Then he came running to tell me he had a new Master, and that he had given him some Ground-nuts already. Then I went along with him to his new Master who told me he loved him: and he should not want. So his new Master carried him away, and I never saw him afterward, till I saw him at Piscataqua..." That was when Joseph was released. Observe how often Mary and her son were allowed to move around the encampments.

The next day Weetamoe's papoose died; this might have been Quanapin's child. Mary was forced out of the wigwam the night before because of the child's sickness. She was then accepted at another wigwam where they "gave me a skin to ly upon, and a mess of Venison and Ground-nuts, which was a choice Dish among them." Mary noted that the papoose's death had the benefit of increasing room in the wigwam.

After "many sorrowful days..." the group moved on the, 14th removal (April 20th) " I have nothing to eat by the way this day, but a few crumbs of Cake, that an Indian gave my grile the same day we were taken." That tells us her daughter did receive some food early on. That day " they killed a Deer, with a young one in her, they gave me a piece of the Fawn, and it was so young and tender, that one might eat the bones as well as the flesh, and yet I thought it was very good." That night it rained, but the wigwam was quickly set up and Mary stayed dry. In the morning, she looked outside and saw that "many" of the Indians had slept outside in the rain and noted that the wetness of those Indians had them "reaking." At this time, she also noted, "Thus the Lord dealt mercifully with me [many] times and I fared better than many of them."

That day, they resumed their travel, and Mary knew they were heading nearer towards her home "...and I went on cheerfully..." That day, she was given a "handfull of Ground-nuts."

"Sometimes one of them would give me a Pipe, another a little Tobacco, another a little Salt: which I would change for a little Victuals." Since she mentions no reason for those gifts, I account it simple generosity.

After a few days on one bank of the Baquaug River, they began to wade across the river. Mary was so cold and weak that she "reeled" in the rapid flow. "...the Indians stood laughing to see me staggering along." To these difficulties, the Indians were hardened, and they enjoyed the English-woman's inferiority in such things. When Mary reached the opposite shore and as she began to travel again, an Indian came to her and informed her she "must go to Wachusit to my Master, for there was a letter come from the [Massachusetts] Council to the Saggamores, about redeeming the Captives..." It was at this time that the Mass. Bay's government was attempting, through the "Praying Indians", to gain the redemption of some of the captives.

That was the day of the16th removal, and there they reached a spot south of the Baquaug River "but [only] one mile [advanced] where they remained two days." While there, a group of horsemen rode into the camp all dressed "in English Apparel." Mary hoped they were really Englishmen, "but when they came near, there was a vast difference between the lovely faces of Christians, and the foul looks of those Heathens which much dampened my spirits again." Beauty and ugliness might be in the eye of the beholder here, but what would Christ think of some of those calling themselves Christians?

The 17th removal brought them to the Indian village of Nichewaug, which must have been unharmed by the English. Mary gave little indication as to whether it was occupied when they arrived there. Mary entered a wigwam where an Indian was boiling horse's feet. When she requested some of the boiling water, "he took a dish, and gave one spoonfull of Samp [ground maize], and bid me take as much of the broth as I would.-He gave me also a piece of the Ruff or Ridding of the small Guts..." Mary gave the Lord credit as usual "...though means be never so inconsiderable, yet if the Lord bestow his blessing upon them, [the nourishments] they shall refresh both Soul and Body." Fortunately for this study of history, Mary did mention the repeated acts of generosity, apparently because she wanted to credit God. We hear of them even if the givers seem unappreciated.

On the 18th removal they reached another Nipmuck town, Wenimeset, near present New Braintree Mass.. Again there was no indication whether native occupied or damaged by the English. They stayed one night there. There were here four English children; one girl was the daughter of Mary's sister- "she was well considering her Captive-condition." The child's masters would not let Mary stay with the child that night. "Then I went into another Wigwam where they were boyling Corn and Beans, which was a lovely sight to see, but I could not get a taste thereof. Then I went into another Wigwam, where there were two of the English children, the Squaw was boyling Horse's feet, then she cut me off a little piece, and gave one of the English Children a piece also. Being very hungry, I had quickly eat up up mine, but the Child could not bite it, it was so tough and sinewy, but lay sucking, gnawing, chewing and slabbering of it ..., then I took it of the Child, and eat it myself, and savoury it was to my taste... Then I went home to my Mistresse's Wigwam; and they told me I disgraced my Master with my begging. And if I did so any more, they would knock me in head: I told them, they had as good knock me in head as starve me to death." We must acknowledge, if true, both Mary's frankness and assertiveness instanced here.

Mary was told, at the time of the 19th removal, that Wachusetts was their goal. It took three days of continuous travel to reach Wachusetts. Wachusetts was the name of the large monadnock in central Massachusetts. On the way there, Philip came up beside Mary and "took me by the hand, and said, Two weeks more and you shall be Mistress again. I asked him if he spoke true? He answered, Yes. And quickly you shall come to your Master again...". Quanapin had been gone for "three weeks". Her next several sentences are presented because they point to Mary's delight in Quanapin's return contrasted to her expressed feelings about Indians who were filthy heathens and followers of the devil. "After many weary steps we came to Wachsetts, where he was: and glad I was to see him. He asked me, When I washt me? I told him not this month, then he fetcht me some water himself, and bid his Squaw get me something to eat: so she gave me a mess of Beans and meat, and a little Ground-nut cake. I was wonderfully revived with the favor shewed me..."

"My Master had three Squaws, living sometimes with one, and sometimes with another ...this old Squaw ["Onux"], at whose Wigwam I was, and with whom my Master had been those three weeks.

Another was Wattimore, [Weetamoe] with whom I had lived and served all this while: A severe and proud Dame she was, bestowing every day in dressing herself neat...powdering her hair, and painting her face, going with Neck-laces, with Jewels in her ears, and Bracelets upon her hands...The third squaw was a younger one, by whom he had two papooses." There was no love between Mary and Weetamoe, obviously.

Soon Weetamoe's maid came and called Mary to return to Weetamoe's wigwam, "at which I fell a weeping...Then the old Squaw told me, to encourage me, that if I wanted victuals, I should come to her, and that I should ly there in her Wigwam. Then I went with the maid,..." but later returned to Onux's wigwam and lodged there. Just how that matter was resolved is not indicated. "The Squaw laid a mat under me, and a good Rugg over me, the first time I had any such kindness shewed me."

Chapter Twenty Two

✦

Elliot's Disciples

Two Praying Indians in the service of Mass.Bay, Nepanet called Tom and Tatatiquinea called Peter, came with another letter from the Mass. Council, dated April 12th concerning the redemption of the captives. These two Indians had been solicited to this duty. Nepanet was "...lately brought down from Concord..." and was solicited by Capt. Henchman to be one of the letter carriers. The council had ordered Major Gookin to try to get some of the Praying Indians of those interred on Deer Island , earlier in the war, to do the same task earlier "...yet I could not prevail with any so that the matter lay dormant a good space of time". {172 Gookin "Hist. Acct."p.507} Tatatiquinea, the other messenger, had a full English name given him, Peter Conway, as if that were an honor.

In a letter from the hostiles brought back by Nepanet and probably received April 12th, 1676 by the English, were these words- "Mr. Rowlandson, your wife and your child is well but one dye. Your sister is well and her three child. John Kittell, your wife and all your child is all well, and all them prisoners taken at Nashua [Lancaster] is all well... This writing by your enemies-Samuel Uskattnhgun [Sagamore Sam] and Gunrashit, two Indian sagamores."{173 Drake "Book of" p.70}

It seems the prospect of trading for the captives had been introduced to the hostiles. The above letter must have been written by a Praying Indian who had learned to write English and may present a more solicitous sentiment than most of the leaders then had. The fact that it is supposedly signed by just two of the leaders may indicate divisiveness in the leaders. If there had been wise and effective leadership of the hostiles, this would have been the time to bring up the question of redemption of natives.

If and when the loved ones of English captives realized their relatives or friends could be freed by the exchange of Indian captives, a damper could occur on the whole process that brought money to the English government from their selling of Indian captives. The Mass. Bay government did not even offer money for Mary's redemption. Mary's ransom was paid by "some Boston Gentlemen and Mrs. Usher". I suspect they did not want to start paying for the captives perhaps realizing it might encourage more captivity. For the Indians, what a chance for justice was missed.

Actually, it has been found in the Mass. State Archives that, in a letter to the captors delivered by Nepanitt (Tom Dublett) dated Mar.13,1676, this dangerous offer was made by the Mass. Bay council as follows; "Inteligence is Come to us, that you have some English (especially woemen and children) in Captivity among you. Wee have therefore sent this messenger offering to redeeme them either for payment in goods or wampum, or by exchange of prisoners."{174 found in Lepore}There can be some doubt as to whether or not such wording "exchange of prisoners" was ever presented to the captors, or if it was so, understood. Whether the captors heard or understood the exchange offer, some of them should have conceived of it themselves. In later years, exchange of prisoners was solicited by Indians and many exchanges did occur. No doubt some discipline on the part of the Indians would have been needed to make captures for exchange; such discipline probably wouldn't have been present in 1676.

For Mary there was joy. The stories of possible redemption, the affirming sign presented by the return nearer to Lancaster and now the letters brought by Nepanet and Tatatiquinea all energized her. "Though they were Indians, I got them by the hand, and burst into tears; my heart was so full that I could not [at first] speak to them,recovering my self, I asked them how my husband did, and all my friends and acquaintance[s]?"

Many of the Indians who surrendered were shipped to the Caribbean living the remainder of their lives in slavery. A few Praying Indians were brought back as a result of the pleading of John Elliot, the preacher to the "Praying Indians", these were either of the Nipmuck or Massachusetts.

Those individuals that the Rev. Elliot had as trusted aids were those he sought. Gookin also managed the return of one Indian.

Without the missionary efforts of John Elliot, known as the "Apostle of the Indians", there would not have been these Praying Indians. His efforts, while not producing truly Puritan Indians, did achieve a partial alienation of the natives of his Praying towns from the cause of the hostiles. That alienation prevented a willingness of those towns to join the hostiles against the English. Most of his towns were established among the Massachusetts, the very people who were the most damaged in the first quarter of the 17th century by the plagues and the attacks by the northern Indians called the Tarrantines. Those disasters made them susceptible to the leadership changes imposed in conjunction with the conversion efforts. I consider Nepanet and Tatatiquinea products or disciples of Elliot.

Elliot had opposed the sale of Indians to the islands both because then there would be no chance to fulfill the mission of bringing them to Christianity, and as he wrote, "to sell souls for money seemeth to me a dangerous merchandize."

Capt. Benjamin Church (considered by many latter writers as the war's hero, certainly so by his son Thomas, who wrote of his father's exploits) originally opposed the selling of captives for the pragmatic reason that future surrenders would not occur when enslavement was know of by otherwise willing Indians. Referring to the surrender of some Indians at Apponagansett (Dartmouth) in July or Aug. 1675 upon a promise of some kind, but sold into slavery, Church wrote - "And had their promise to the Indians been kept, and the Indians fairly treated, it is probable that most, if not all, the Indians in those parts had soon followed the example of those who had now surrendered themselves, which would have been a good step towards finishing the war."{175 Church p.57} Perhaps so, since so many Indians did seem to be reluctant to enter battle. However, Church offered an even better strategy in late 1676, when he offered amnesty to any Indian men and their families, if those men would join him in capturing other Indians. Shamefully, many may have. Church also made other promises to induce Indians to surrender, promises that his son's writing indicates he was unable to see kept, i.e., Anawan, Tispaquin. {176 Church p.144-146}

Chapter Twenty Three

✦

Advantages and Disadvantages

In this war both sides had advantages and disadvantages. The English had the advantage of their stockade houses to which English could flee in an attack and survive with ammunition and food stocked therein. The Indians could flee into the woods where the English could only follow with difficulty and danger of ambush. Both sides each destroyed the other's crops. The English could obtain some supplies of food from distant ports. The hostiles did obtain food through slaughter and theft of English livestock, through hunting and foraging in the wild, and from hidden and below ground caches of maize.

The English had a large advantage in supply of shot and powder; it is a wonder that the natives had as much as they seem to have had. Patrick Malone wrote; "The Indians learned the art of casting in lead, pewter and brass soon after the establishment of colonies in New England."{177 Malone p.70} However, "One skill which the Indians lacked and wanted desperately, was the making of gun-powder."{178 Malone p.72} A low supply of powder may have been a reason for the thoughts of surrender. The English seemed to have guns for all able-bodied men, whereas some accounts indicate some Indians did not have functioning guns. However, the Indians managed to get flintlock rifles. Malone wrote; "Despite increasing evidence that the matchlock [rifle] was unsuited for forest warfare, colonial governments were slow requiring militiamen to equip themselves with expensive flintlocks… the average Indian was quicker to realize this [advantage in forest warfare] than the average colonist." The sale of guns and powder was both banned and allowed at different times and that because the sale or trade of those was so difficult to prevent. The use of bow and arrow is seldom mentioned. Malone notes "the New England bows were not powerful, but at moderate range they could easily kill a man."{179 Malone p.35}

The English had the great advantages of organization, planning, supplies, and a highly motivated colonial population facing loss of livelihood and with little option but to follow the directives of their leaders. Those leaders seem to have been fairly competent men selected from the general body by church attending males. Whereas the natives had, or thought they had, the option of exiting the struggle, at least on the clan or village level. They had no one great leader whom they loyally followed. The English offered "...whatsoever Indians should... come in to the English might hope for Mercy" {180 Hubbard p.249} The Indians offered nothing to the English that we know of.

In the eighty-two days that Mary was a captive, there were reports in contemporary accounts of forty attacks on settlements in Mass. Bay, Plymouth and Rhode Island. These attacks ranged from the burning of a few houses and barns to attacks extensive enough to cause loss of dozens of lives and /or to cause the abandonment of some settlements. Sometimes settlements were only abandoned after two or more attacks, while some small settlements, out of fear, were abandoned before any attack. The island of Aquidneck (then called Rhode Island) was crowded with settlers who had fled other towns. Church fled there with his family from his house in Sekonnet. Aquidneck was a safe haven; no move was made upon it by the natives. One contemporary writer wrote that some English contemplated that all of New England might be forced to flee to various islands off of the coast as the situation worsened. In most of southern New England and Maine and New Hampshire in 1676, colonists were afraid to travel between towns. Even going outside of dwellings to perform needed tasks in small numbers was fearful. William Harris, Warwick R.I. resident/owner, wrote, "ther is noe safe Sending nor passing to & fro..." [from place to place]. Many of the settlers were so frightened in the spring of 1676 that they were abandoning their homes rather than risking being killed or captured there. The government of Mass. Bay passed laws trying to discourage such abandonment by threatening confiscation of abandoned property if done so without permission. Yet, Mass. Bay on April 1, 1676, ordered Major Savage to move most of his troops from the valley back to the east in order to have greater numbers there with no more than 150 left to help defend all the towns in the valley.

In about Oct.1675, the Mass. Bay secretary wrote this to John Pynchon, leader of Springfield in the valley: "The slaughter in your parts has much dampened many spirits [because] of the war. Some men escape away from the press, and others hide away after they are impressed." Maj. Simon Willard, in a letter to the Council, Jan. 29, 1676, wrote, "...I thought it not meet to release men, when we stand in need of men, my desire is to know what I shall do here in Concord and chelmford [concerning his 100 or so troops] [they] look every day to be fired, and would have more men but know not how to keep them, nor pay them, your humble servant."

Each town had to raise a certain number of men to fill their quota of forces raised. Some men fled from their own towns to avoid being impressed. Laws were passed allowing the town wherein they might be found could force them to be used as part of the quota of that town.

In Plymouth, so many of the men pressed failed to go forth that the March campaign had to be canceled. One Robert Baker was broken as a lieutenant and fined for desertion, as were sixteen men who joined him. {P.C.R.}The cost of pay of militiamen became too great for Plymouth, and a force raised to serve under Capt Church was told that their pay would be determined on the basis of their receiving one half of the value of the enslaved captives. With that method, any Indian, neutral or not, was liable to be captured.

The overall situation for the English in the spring of 1676 was that the citizenry was very anxious and moving toward revolting. The situation for the Indians was also probably bad, but would it be especially so in that spring? Rather it seemed the spirit of the movement disappeared by mid -summer 1676. It was then that some of the Connecticut river tribes responded positively to overtures made to them by Conn., or the tribes themselves made the overtures. Perhaps some of the Nipmuck tribes thought they also might get some kind of accommodation with Mass. Bay. What a foolish mistake! Did they think they could kill Englishmen and accept their vague offer of some kind of peace? How many Indians would find a noose around their neck on Boston Common for their foolish acceptance in June of Mass.

Bay's offer - "that whatsoever Indians should within 14 Days...come in to the English might hope for Mercy."{181 Hubbard p.249}

But what were the difficulties experienced by the Indians? Mary Rowlandson noted that, after the attack of Sudbury April,1676, the Indians told her that they had lost but "five or six". This was when seventy or more English were killed. Yet from this encampment of Indians were those who later sought peace.

Reports of Indian losses by contemporary writers are always suspect because they are seldom able to really ascertain Indian losses but are glad to present large numbers as the Indian losses. The likelihood of the giving of exaggerated figures for Indian losses prevents any reasonable assessment of the effects of losses upon the mood of the general body of the hostile Indians. Were the losses seen as devastating or were they only noticed by Indians near the location of the loss? Some of those reports however should be entered here.

Hubbard claimed eighty Indians were killed or wounded on the attack of Brookfield on about Aug.6, 1675. {182 Hubbard p.99-104}. Conn. river Indians were overtaken Aug 26 ,ten miles north of Hatfield and twenty-six Indians were killed.{183 Ibid p.109} In the ambush of Capt. Lathrop, Sept.18, 1675 there were killed ninety-six Indians. {184 Ibid p.118 } In Dec.1675, there was the attack upon the Narragansett country, including the "Great Swamp Fight." I. Mather stated that perhaps one thousand Indian souls were killed that day and more later on plus the destruction of several villages. {185 I. Mather p.116} From Gov. Andros - "...the latter end of Feb.[1676] [the Hodosonee] fell upon, killed and took several, and drove said Philip and other Indians with him quite away, and since kept continuall partyes out to free the coasts towards us [N.Y.] and prevent old Indyans recourse to Canada."{186 Jennings p.315 /N.Y. Col. Doc.}

The English invasion upon the Narragansetts in Dec.1675 could not have contributed to the discouragement of the Nipmuck or the Connecticut River tribes who were the ones who later in part, responded to the vague offers by the English. That invasion was what caused the Narragansetts to enter the war and must have invigorated the Indian side. There is no telling when, if ever, the Narragansetts would have joined the hostiles without having that invasion occur.

Mar.29, 1676, the Indians attacked Northhampton. The town was full of soldiers and the Indians were "quickly repulsed" with "the lose of many." {187 Hubbard p.205} Capt. Brattle's troops killed eleven or twelve Indians near Rehoboth in Mar. 1676. {188 Ibid p.226} Mar.29, Capt. Denison with English, Pequots, Mohegans and Niantics operating in the Narragansett country, killed and took forty-five Indians amongst whom was Canonchet, the premier sachem of the Narragansetts.

Canonchet's capture and execution certainly could have been a considerable discouragement to all of the hostiles. It is recorded that he was overtaken as he fled an attack by Denison's party, overtaken by a Pequot brave as Canonchet fled alone. How could such a sachem be allowed to flee alone? How could the Pequots assist the English so effectively when the English had tried to destroy the Pequots as a tribe forty years before? The answer to that second question may be – the patronage of Gov. John Winthrop Jr., but how is that answer really sufficient? There are indications, in some accounts, that there was long standing enmity between the Pequots and the Narragansetts but it is certain that the Pequots were able to go to the Narragansetts with some hope of having them support them in their troubles with Connecticut in 1635.

Some later historians have asserted that Canonchet was the greatest leader of the Indians in King Philip's War, but they never present any evidence for that. Few of any of the sachems are ever identified in the attacks and battles, and, as in all conflicts, the leaders are usually shielded from the enemy.

Hubbard apparently could not resist fabricating a story about Canonchet's capture; "with about thirty Men" Canonchet was found at "some Wigwams not far from Pawtucket...in one of which [he]... was at that Moment divertizing himself, with the Recital of Capt. Pierce's Slaughter...by his Men a Few Days before..."{189 Hubbard – post script p.56} Capt. Pierce, with fifty English and twenty Cape Cod Wampanoag, had been ambushed near Pawtucket; nearly all were killed "...some Few made their escape ..." That happened on Mar.26, 1676. {190 Hubbard p.172&180} Hubbard does not come up with an explanation of how it was known that Canonchet was "divertizing" about anything at that time, and his often used explanation "of that we were informed by captives later" was not added here to make his story sound believable.

The destruction of Warwick was completed about Mar.16, 1676, Thirty barns and forty houses were destroyed in Rehoboth on Mar.28, and Providence had fifty-four houses burned and was abandoned on about Mar.29. {191 Hubbard p.179& P. Script X11&p.47} "The like Mischief was acted...upon the Houses of the English in the Narragansett Country." {192 Hubbard p.179} These attacks all occurred in March in the area near to Pierce's destruction and Canonchet's capture. Thus it seems likely that the Indians whom Canonchet probably led made those several assaults there, but that hardly makes him the great leader of the war.

On Mar. 28, the inhabitants of Sudbury gathered a force of about forty and fell upon a parcel of Indians then sleeping at a spot about a half a mile from the garrison, wounding forty of which fourteen died. {193 Hubbard p.208} In late March, Conn. "Capt. G. Denison with fifty-six volunteers and one hundred and twelve Pequots killed and took prisoners seventy-six, amongst whom were two Narragansett sachems..."{194 Hubbard p.183} On May 6 an English force of horse and foot "met with a considerable Party of the Enemy, they were first discovered by the Natick scouts...[and] fell upon them...killed and took...about fifteen." {195 Hubbard p.224}

In the attack occurring on May 18[th,] referred to earlier, at Peskeompskut (since called Turner's Falls), more than one hundred and fifty English fell upon the sleeping Indian encampment there. Hubbard wrote- "such as came back [claimed]...of the Number of the Slain... there could not in Reason be less than two or three hundred..." This was followed by the Indian counterstrike in which Capt. Turner and thirty-eight of his men were killed. {196 Hubbard p.229}

Those preceding losses could possibly have caused the hostiles to consider ending hostilities. We can't known if it were so, we can only speculate. The timing of Mary's redemption, May 2nd, the release of other English captives and the consideration of some Nipmucks to approach the English are notable.

Chapter Twenty-Four

✦

Praying Indians

It was April 28th when Mary's party reached the encampment where Quanapin was, and until that date at least, it still seemed the hostiles were winning the war despite the losses claimed by the English When the letter from Boston via the two Praying Indians was deciphered, "the sagamores" called Mary to come before them saying "they were the General Court" (a rather healthy perception and parody of the English pretense of proper authority) and asked "how much her husband would give to redeem me." Mary thought wisely and perhaps cleverly that- "I was in a great strait: I thought if I should speak of but a little, it would be slighted, and hinder the matter, if of a great sum, I know not where it would be procured: yet at a venture, I said Twenty pounds, yet desired them to take less; but they would not hear of that, but sent that message to Boston, that for Twenty pounds I should be redeemed." One Peter Jethro not Peter Conway, a Praying Indian wrote a letter to Boston asking for the twenty pounds. Whether that Praying Indian was loyal to Hostiles or to the English service is not stated. The Indians from the Praying towns were of mixed allegiances, some working for the English and some fighting against them, and probably many switched sides, especially toward the end of the war.

Praying Indians were so called by the English because they were semi-Christianized and had been taught some prayers. Only a few were considered fully converted, but the effort at Christianizing villages did accomplish something for the English purposes. This effort undermined the natives sense of their own values and tended to impose English values. The effort was combined with a dispossession of the natural leaders and the imposition of leaders chosen by the English. The Narragansetts, the Mohegans and most of the Wampanoag and some of the Nipmuck were unapproachable to the missionary efforts. Neil Salisbury wrote- "Charles II's commissioners after their visit to New England in 1664, charged that the missionaries were doing nothing for the natives except to undermine their traditional structure of authority".{197 Salisbury p.201} Further he wrote; "The red man's position within the Puritan church mirrored his dependent, subordinate position within the larger society".{198Salisbury p.229}

Major Daniel Gookin, chosen as the ruler over the Praying Indians in 1656 and himself a Puritan, made an interesting observation of the Quakers that really suits well the Puritan missionary efforts. He tells of the landing on the island of Martha's Vineyard of some Quakers, who tried to convert the Indians there. He says they were rejected by those Indians. "So the Quakers not long after departed from the island, and never since have they been infested with them". {199 Gookin"Hist. Coll." p.63} Indeed the Puritans infested the Praying Indians and because of that many of them provided the English with invaluable assistance and guidance in King Philip's War.

Yet, almost all the colonists distrusted all the Indians, praying or non-praying. Exposed to anti-Indian bigotry and rhetoric as they were, a conscious or unconscious fear that the people they were taking land from could at some time turn on them and a concept of savagery were sufficient reasons for distrust. Despite the efforts of the Rev. John Elliot and Gookin to gain appreciation for the Praying Indians by the general body of the colonists, most of them were shipped early in the war to Deer Island in Massachusetts Bay. Later in the war, they were brought in to assist in the war.

Chapter-Twenty five

✦

The Discouraging Victory

It was about the end of April when Mary was interviewed by the Indian leaders. During that time, a large attack was made on Sudbury on Apr. 18th by those same Indians who held Mary. The attack caused much death and destruction at Sudbury. Mary's observation of the apparent mood of the Indians before and after the attack is really significant. "To my thinking they went out without any scruple, but that they should prosper, and gain the victory. And they went out not so rejoycing, but they came home with as great a Victory. For they said they had killed two Captains, an almost an hundred men.

One Englishman they brought along with them: and he said, it was too true, for they had made sad work at Sudbury, as indeed it proved. Yet they came home without that rejoycing and triumphing over their victory, which they were wont to show at other times, but rather like Dogs (as they say) which have lost their ears. Yet I could not perceive that it was for their own loss of men: They said they had not lost above five or six: and I missed none, except in one Wigwam." Mary would only have seen her own encampment; perhaps other encampments may have existed and joined in the attack and sustained losses also. I. Mather wrote this of the Sudbury attack- "...a Captive since escaped out of their hands, affirms that the Indians said one to another, that they had an hundred and twenty fighting men kill'd this day."{200 I. Mather p.116}

Mary continued- "When they went, they acted as if the Devil had told them they should gain the victory: and now they acted, as if the Devil had told them they should have a fall. Whither it were so or no, I cannot tell, but so it proved, for quickly they began to fall, and so held on that Summer, till they came to utter ruine." Did the Indians see a bad omen in the happenings at Sudbury? Did a revered Powaw meet death there? Did just one Indian see something in the sky that day, a bad omen that he or she passed on to others that day? These were suspicious people, and something may have happened that changed the mood of these Indians dramatically. The record does seem to change after Sudbury at least for central Mass. Bay where this particular body of Indians was. There were assaults into the summer in Plymouth Colony, (these seems to be by Nemaskets and other Wampanoags) and upon Connecticut River towns by Connecticut River tribes. Otherwise the offensive seems to have been dropped by most of the hostiles.

Also at about this time, the Mohawks became active against the hostiles. I. Mather wrote "...a Letter came from Connecticut to Boston [May 10], informing that God had let loose the Mohawks upon our Enemies, and that they were sick of Fluxes and Fevers..." {201 I. Mather p.118}. Actually, it was Governor Andros who wrote to Connecticut that he had set off the Mohawks, but Mather did not wish to give credit to Andros.

This decrease in activities by the hostiles allowed the English to reduce their defensive posture and gave the average English soldier new courage.

Gookin wrote "This treaty about the captives" wherein "...Mrs. Rowlandson and some others were redeemed ...and the consequences thereof, had no small influence into the abatement of the enemy's violence and our troubles, and had a tendency to dividing them and break their union, and consequently their strength; for Philip and some other of the enemy's chief men were utterly against treating with the English or surrendering the captives...[but other Indians] would mollify the Englishmen's minds in order to a peace. This contest about the treaty, caused them to fall out and divide. Philip and most of the Narragansett Indians separated from the inland Indians and went down into their own country, and the inland Indians staid about Wachuset mountain; which was a means under God to weaken and destroy them...This was another piece of service done by our Praying Indians; at least they broke the ice...by their first adventuring to treat with the enemy."

"In this juncture of affairs, the Council at last resolved to arm and send forth a company of Praying Indians from Deer Island, under... Samuel Hunting...Upon the 21ˢᵗ of April, Capt. Hunting had drawn up and ready furnished his company of forty Indians at Charlestown."{202 Gookin "Hist. Acct." p.508} Gookin also noted that the English were able to arm all of the Praying Indians "up to the number of eighty men", this after the arrival of supplies in ships from England in May 1676.{203 Ibid p.512}

Gookin desired to tell of the essential aid given by his Indians which can be seen is largely true. It is also possible that the Praying Indians encouraged their friends among the hostiles to seek peace at that time.

Chapter Twenty-Six

◆

A "General Court"

"About this time there came an Indian to me and bid me to come to his Wigwam, at night, and he would give me some Pork and Ground-Nuts. Which I did, and as I was eating, another Indian said to me, he seems to be your good Friend, but he killed two Englishmen at Sudbury, and there ly their Cloaths behind you: I looked behind me, and there I saw bloody Cloaths, with Bullet-holes in them; yet the Lord suffered not this wretch to do me any hurt; Yeh, instead of that, he many times refresht me: five or six times did he and his Squaw refresh my feeble carcass. If I went to their Wigwam at any time, they would always give me something, and yet they were strangers that I never saw before. Another Squaw gave me a piece of Pork, and a little Salt with it, and lent me her Pan to Fry it in; and I cannot but remember what a sweet, pleasant and delightful relish that bit had to me, to this day."

The next remove, about April 28th, was to a spot near the southern end of the lake near Mt. Wachusett "My sister being not far from the place where we now were, and hearing that I was here, desired her master to let her come and see me, and he was willing to it, and would go with her: but she being ready before him, told him she would go on before, and was come within a Mile or two of the place; Then he overtook her, and began to rant as if he were mad; and made her go back again in the Rain; so that I never saw her till I saw her in Charlestown."

Mary's sister's master was said to be Uskutugun, known as Sagamore Sam. Now, why would he allow his captive to wander off alone at all. The sister must have been used to too much freedom, and there could have been a communication problem.

Mary complained of not being allowed to see either her daughter, who "...was...about a mile off" or her sister, also nearby. What about those Indian captives sent to the Caribbean never to see their native land again and possibly loved ones as well?

Soon, one John Hoar of Concord arrived at the encampment with the same two Praying Indians, "Tom and Peter" who had been the carriers of the previous letters, with the third letter from Boston and with the ransom. Hoar was taken to the sagamores (chiefs in the north were called sagamores in the south, sachems) with whom he conferred, and when that was done, Mary was allowed to talk with him.

Mary asked some Indians if she could now leave with Hoar, and she was told no. The following morning, Hoar invited the sagamores to dinner, "but when we went to get it ready, we found that they had stolen the greatest part of the Provision Mr. Hoar had brought, out of his Bags, in the night. And we may see the wonderfull power of God, in that one passage, in that when there was such a great number of Indians together, and so greedy of a little good food; and no English there, but Mr. Hoar and myself; that they did not knock us in the head, and take what we had: there being not only some Provision, but also some Trading-cloth, a part of the twenty pounds agreed upon: But instead of doing us any mischief, they seemed to be ashamed of the fact, and said, it were some Matchit [bad or bad behaving] Indian that did it. Oh, that we could believe that there is no thing too hard for God! God shewed his Power over the Heathen in this..." There certainly must have been temptation to steal that food. Again Mary credited God for the decency and the embarrassment of the chiefs. This prevented her from recognizing a virtue in their culture, or perhaps, enabled her not to recognize it.

After Hoar and Mary prepared and served a meal to some of the sagamores, the Indians held a great dance lasting almost until night. Some time after the dance, Quanapin sent the Praying Indian "James the Printer" into the wigwam of Mary and Hoar with his message, "...that my Master would let me go home to morrow, if he [Hoar] would let him have one pint of Liquors. Then Mr. Hoar called his own Indians, Tom and Peter and bid them go and see whither he would promise it before them three: and if he would, he should have it; which he did, and he had it...My Master after he had his drink, quickly came ranting into the

Wigwam again, and called for Mr.Hoar, drinking to him, and saying, He was a good man: and then again he would say, Hang him Rogue: Being almost drunk, he would drink to him, and yet presently say he should be hanged. Then he called for me. I trembled to hear, yet I was fain to go to him, and he drank to me, shewing no incivility. He was the first Indian I saw drunk all the while that I was amongst them. [lack of easy access certainly, perhaps some discipline, but Quanapin apparently knew of the mood altering power of alcohol] At last his squaw ran out, and he after her, round the Wigwam, with his money jingling at his knees: But she escaped him: But (also) having an old squaw he ran to her..." From this, we know Quanapin had sexual desires, but Mary never let the reader think it was ever directed towards her.

Seemingly just prior to this, Philip called Mary to him "and asked me what I would give him, to tell me some good news, and speak a good word for me." He even specified what he wanted "two Coats and twenty shillings in Mony, and half a bushel of seed Corn, and some Tobacco." Mary handled this cleverly, not saying to him that she already knew the "good news", but saying that she had nothing she could offer, and noting that he was "the crafty Fox".

"On Tuesday morning [May 1st ?] they called their General Court (as they call it) to consult and determine, whether I should go home; except Philip, who would not come among them."

Philip should be credited as being correct on opposing the release of Mary or any other captives if he did so on the basis of what was obtained or not obtained by the release. The captives had been a extra drain on the Indian's resources for weeks. What value did they gain in Mary's case- some clothes, and some probably useless English coins? Clothing was often obtained from slain English, and where would they be able to use English money? The release process in any of these releases could create dissension between those who considered the captives theirs and the others who knew the captives were taken in joint efforts, risks and sacrifices. The release of captives should have benefited in some way the whole effort of the Indians to redeem their independence, freedom and land. As mentioned before, demanding exchange of English for Indian captives had value, even if not in fact accomplished. Such bargaining could raise the specter of the injustice of the English enslavements in the common Englishman's mind, especially if their own loved one's were captives.

But Philip's offer to Mary speaks poorly of his designs. This was the man who was in the best position to lead this struggle against the usurpers, but he was just a man with no training or special aptitude for the role. We know of nothing that indicates the war-making ability of this sachem of the village of Montaup/Sowams or of its' people or that of any hostile sachem. At the beginning of the war, Philip had to lead the pursuing English army into the lands of his reluctant neighboring Wampanoag villages of Poccaset and Sekonnet to involve them in the conflict. They would soon abandon Philip after Nipsachuck, only to rejoin the fight when their Narragansett succorers were themselves invaded by the English in December 1675.

Chapter Twenty-Seven

✦

Wampanoag Sachems

Philip became sachem in 1662 as the next in line in the family that provided the sachems of his village, also with some kind of supposed authority over all the other Wampanoag villages. The English called such sachems "supreme sachems", but it seems villages did pretty much what they chose to do as best suited their own village interests. Philip's older brother Wamsutta, named Alexander by the Plymouth government, died under circumstances of interrogation and possible coercion after being arrested by Plymouth. Wamsutta came under suspicion by Plymouth shortly after his father (or grandfather) Massasoit died in 1662.

Betty Grofff Schroeder wrote in her work, "The True Lineage of King Philip," that Philip was actually the son of one Moanam, who was a son of Massasoit. "Moanam had died while Massasoit, his father was still sachem...Indian custom denotes that mentioning the dead is disrespectful, so it is understandable why Moanam's name has been lost to historians..." {204 Schroeder}

While Massasoit lived, Plymouth held him in great trust based on his early acceptance of their presence, and he never seemed to have done anything to alter Plymouth's confidence in him. But it is not surprising that a new sachem would be viewed differently, as almost any Indian was subject to English suspicion. The general opinion of the English was that Indians were not to be trusted, and further, the colonists consciously or unconsciously, feared that the natives would, at some time, resist the taking of the land.

It had been reported that Wamsutta had been talking to the Narragansetts and that a combination of the two peoples would be a strong threat to the English. It was perfectly fine for the Puritan colonies to have their own regular meeting of the United Colonies, established for their mutual defense and offense as practiced in the Pequot War, but any talking between tribes was cause for alarm. It was also alright for Plymouth to assemble a body of magistrates as early as 1671 which they titled "the Council of War". One direction given to its'members was- "...you shall faithfully keep cecrett [secret] all such expeditions and achieuements as may or shalbe ordered and contriued by the council of war..." a second directive was "...you shall with like cecresye conceale all other matters that may be agitated...by the said council..." {205 Shurtleft/Ply.Records vol.V p.64} Surely it was from the Indians that its' plans were to be kept secret. This Council of War was active in the spring of 1671. {Ibid p.76} It was also in 1671 that Plymouth made efforts to alienate each Wampanoag village from Philip's Pokanoket.

Ben Church, in, it seems June of 1675, went to confer with Awashonks the squaw-sachem of Sakonnet with the object of drawing her away from any alliance with Philip. This Council of War must have kept its planning secret from their quasi-ambassador or else he Church was disingenuous when he made this statement to Awashonks- "Then he told her [Awashonk] it was but a few days since he came from Plymouth, and the English were making no preparations for war; that he was in company with the principal gentlemen of the government, who had no discourse at all about war, and he believed no thoughts about it." {206 Church p.23}. See Chapter 28 – The Council of War was sending some Cape Indians into slavery in August of 1675 because they failed to reveal Philip's plans.

It was well for the Indians to mock the English General Court but it would have been better to have gleaned an understanding of the mentality of a neighbor that formed a "secret" "Council of War" plotting their control.

The court at Plymouth on March 1, 1675 had threatened the sachem of the Wampanoag village of Nemasket with the loss of 100 pounds worth of Nemasket land if he did not cause Tobias to appear in Plymouth's court. This may be how Tobias was brought to Plymouth where he was tried and executed for the alleged murder of Sassamon. We can suspect that Plymouth had no intention of making war as long as coercion of Indians made that unnecessary.

From 1671 on Plymouth worked, apparently with mixed success, to alienate most Wampanoag villages from whatever allegiance they had to Philip.

Not only did the English fear alliance of tribes, they also sought to peel-off villages from ties they had with other villages. Even when John Easton, Lt. Gov. of R.I., and a Quaker, criticized in his "Relation..." Plymouth's pressure put upon Philip in the last year, he also mentioned approvingly R.I.'s efforts to split Weetamoe's Pocassets from Philip.

The claimed submission of the supreme-sachem Massasoit to the English king gave Plymouth pretended claim to all Wampanoag land, land that extended eastward from Narragansett Bay to the ocean and from the ocean north to some vague line some twenty miles south of Boston.

Plymouth got itself involved in the untimely death of Wamsutta by first demanding he appear at Plymouth to explain his talks with the Narragansetts. When he failed to appear, an armed force was sent to apprehend him. The stories provided by Mather and Hubbard tell that Major Winslow, was sent to Sowams, but accidentally found Wamsutta at a hunting spot not far from Plymouth. Winslow bravely demanded Wamsutta return with them to meet with the governor at Plymouth, even though Wamsutta has either "eighty" armed men (Hubbard) or "many" armed men (Mather). Wamsutta finally agrees to go, but Gov. Prince was not then at Plymouth but at his home at Eastham forty or so miles from there. Wamsutta became ill while in custody and was released before seeing the governor. He dies shortly thereafter, either on his way home or after reaching Sowams.{207 Hubbard p.50,& I. Mather }.The Rev. John Cotton, after reading Mather's story, wrote to him and cautioned him that "...there are many mistakes..." therein which Major Bradford, himself in the arresting party, revealed to Cotton. Cotton wrote that "they found Alexander with about eight men and sundry squaws...at Munponset River..." nearby to Plymouth. Wamsutta was eating breakfast, guns aside. Bradford wrote that Wamsutta provided a reason for not going to Plymouth upon their first request as he had desired to talk with Capt. Willet of Swansea before going to Plymouth. But now Wamsutta "freely and readily consented to go..." to Plymouth where he spoke with "...the few Magistrates..." and was, after that, peaceably dismissed. Mather's and Hubbard's stories further present Wamsutta as fully upset and angry but soon wilting in the face of English courage. Cotton's letter, discovered later, proves the two historians had misinformation or fabricated their stories. {208 Drake B. of I. P8} Why would the Rev. Cotton be concerned with the truth of Mather's story? Perhaps he was a strong believer in the truth, or perhaps he cared that other Englishmen who knew those events correctly would promote scoffing at the two reverend's histories. Perhaps he recognized the importance of the story of the arrest, the following suspicious death of Wamsutta and how the death may have led to such disastrous subsequent events.

The stories presented of those events by the two primary historians of the war could be simply misinformation but are more likely to be more fabrications fueled by a hatred of the "savages". Such fabrications, when and if they occur, debase the Indians and help to justify their destruction.

A more significant effect of the arrest and the death of Wamsutta would be in the minds of his own people who heard the story provided by those Indians who had been with Wamsutta. Was he poisoned? It may have been believed that, in some way, he was. His arrest had to be seen as a hostile act, followed by his becoming ill while detained and then dying.

Poisoning may have been suspected decades earlier when some Cape Cod sachems became sick and died after they were suspected of plotting against Plymouth in 1623. Those deaths occurred following the execution of an aggressive plan by Plymouth against some Massachusetts Indians, which became an assassination.

Myles Standish and his party of nine men journeyed in March 1623 to the plantation of John Weston located just south of present-day Boston. Edward Winslow wrote; "...we came to this conclusion, that Standish should take so many men , as he thought sufficient to make ...good against all the Indians in Massachusetts Bay..., he should pretend trade, as at other times; but first go to the English [there] and acquaint them with the plot..." When he arrived "Standish asked them how they durst...live in such [lack of] security; who answered, they feared not the Indians, but lived and suffered them to lodge with them, not having sword or gun, or needing the same." The response from the English living there did not deter Standish from his mission.

"On the next day [Mar.26?], seeing he [Standish]could not get many of them [Indians] together at once, and this Pecksuot and Wituwamat together, with another man, and a youth of 18...brother of Wituwamat and villan-like [also]" got those four and it seems some Indian women "...in a room...and the doors being shut- having about as many of his own [inside]...gave the word to his men" they drew knives and killed the males. Standish brought back the head of Wituwamat "...being brought to the fort [at Plymouth] and there set up...to bring terror to the hearts of all Indians with like plans." Those "plans" would only be Plymouth's suspicion of a plot by Indians against them. It certainly does not sound as if this Wituwamat was thinking of attacking Plymouth when we read that he was at the plantation to trade along with a younger brother, two other males and women.

There had been stories of some of settlers at Weston's plantation being abused by some of the Massachusett Indians there. I submit that such happenings caused anxiety in Plymouth and were intolerable to the leaders there, but those English at Weston's did not want Plymouth's help. It was an audacious act to attempt killing of some of the Massachusetts Indians thereby inviting retaliation from the whole tribe, which however, did not happen. Plymouth's leaders with their mentality, likely felt justified in their actions but the words from Weston's people indicates that it was not. By mentality here, I mean Plymouth intended to intimidate these savage people by whatever means they thought would work, whenever they saw a possible threat. Assassinating those who may not have done any wrong, while wrong itself, was not as important as intimidating possible enemies.

Winslow wrote further- "Concerning those other people, that intended to join the Massacheuseuks against us, though we never went out against them; yet this sudden and unexpected execution, together with the best judgment of God...hath so terrified and amazed them, as in like manner they forsooktheir houses...living in swamps and other desert places...whereof very many are dead, as Canacum the sachem of Manomet, Aspinet...of Nauset and Ianough...of Mattachiest."{210 Winslow p.43-50}The sudden death of these sachems after the killing of several Massachusetts could have caused suspicion of their being poisoned. Wamsutta's death in 1662 certainly could have looked like poisoning to his people.

It is unlikely that Plymouth would in any way plan to harm Wamsutta. Most likely, they intended to size him up, intimidate him and possibly coerce some agreement from him. Their action and his death muddied the waters, and into these waters stepped Wamsutta's younger brother, Pometacom/Philip.

Philip was probably in his mid-twenties when he became sachem in 1662. He faced immediate suspicion by Plymouth, and he must have had very negative feelings toward Plymouth. The entire situation between the Wampanoag and the English certainly should have seemed intolerable to any thinking Wampanoag.

The expansion of the English was insatiable. Everywhere, throughout what the four colonies considered their domain, land sales and land acquisitions continued to proceed unabated. New settlers came in from England each year, (there was an abatement of Puritan migration for a while after the English Civil War) most hoping for land. English colonial families were large, and widows and widowers were quickly remarried and producing more children.

Was Philip plotting with other Indian villages? It does seem he was trying to find out who would join him in an uprising. Violence of sufficient degree was the only way the native people could hope to dislodge the English or force them to a small submissive population and enable the natives to keep the type of life that seemed to have always been theirs.

There were a number of problems faced by Philip or any Indian leader trying to gather a group of villages willing to take on the rather large English population in New England, which by 1670 was estimated at 52,000, most in southern New England. Those problems were:

1. His plans if there were any, had to be made in secret since any hint of such plans was certain to bring quick English reaction. There were many individual Indians who were willing to carry information to the English in order to ingratiate themselves. Others such as Ninigret, the sachem of the Niantics, was so intimidated by the English in earlier times as to be a tale - carrier to them. He actually told them that Philip was plotting;

2. The English were suspicious of any sachem of any relatively large village such as Philip's village and ;

3. The apparent sentiment among many natives was against war.

An example of another significant Indian carrying tales to the English was Wauban, a leader of the Praying town of Natick, who, in April of 1675, "came to one of the magistrates on purpose, and informed him that he had grounds to fear that Philip intended some mischief shortly..." this per Gookin {211 Drake "B.of I"p.14} The most significant snitch was John Sassamon, a Praying Indian of the Massachusetts, who had worked for Philip as his secretary and translator but left that role and was living at Assawampset neck on Assawampset Pond. {212 Ibid p.9} He reportedly told the governor of Plymouth in 1674 that Philip had been plotting for war. His dead body was found that winter under the ice of that pond. {213 I. Mather "Brief"p.87}

A story of his murder was revealed, conveniently for Plymouth's purposes, by another Indian who while hiding nearby, saw three of "Philip's" men kill Sassamon and place his body under the ice. Again conveniently, Plymouth apprehended the three, tried and convicted them. The three were strung up to be hung, but the rope for one of them broke. That one then confesses that they all did the deed, and he is later shot.

Philip was said to have stated that Plymouth should have had nothing to do with Indians killing other Indians, thereby attacking Plymouth's pretended authority. Nowhere, however, is it written that Philip claimed that the three did not do it.

Plymouth tells us, via their histories, that Massasoit, the supreme sachem of the Wampanoags, had early on submitted himself, his people and all their lands to them as agents of the king, giving Plymouth authority. Again we read and understand (and most believe) the language of the writers, while the Wampanoag did not.

If the death of Sassamon was perceived as an execution ordered by Philip, it would have sent a message to would - be collaborators not to carry information damaging to Philip to Plymouth. The same perception, taken by Plymouth, would require a counter – strike. The execution of the three "Mt. Hope" men would be such a counter-strike and assert Plymouth's authority and power.

After the executions of the three Indians, Philip and many of his people may have become frightened and or angered by the act. Many historians suspect hostilities then developed prematurely for Philip. More preparations for a general war would have been needed to have hope of eventual success. Tensions did increase, and rumors of war caused most homes in Swansea (where the English had built upon lands used by the villages of Sowams and Pocasset, Philip's and Weetamoe's villages) to be vacated on or about June 18, 1675. Some Mt. Hope/ Sowams Indians looted some of those houses. One of the homeowners shot and killed one of the looters. The Indians responded "immediately" on June 24th killing nine or so English that day. {214Hubbard p.64} Easton's story in Chapter 2 suggests a different sequence.

For Philip there was no turning back after that day. Nor was there turning back for Canonchet, Pumham, Pessacus or Quanapin after the United Colonies' invasion of the Narragansett country in Dec.1675 when they were virtually forced into the conflict. Many of the Nipmuck and Connecticut River tribes mistakenly thought they could turn back however.

Chapter Twenty-Eight

✦

Strengths

Did Philip ever really have a chance of overcoming the colonists of New England? Beer wrote- "In 1671, the Earl of Sandwich... 'President of the Council for Plantations'" expressed his thoughts thusly - "New England was already at that date... a numerous and thriving people and in twenty years was likely 'to be mighty, rich and powerful and not at all careful of their dependence upon old England.'... Sandwich realized that it was impossible 'to prevent wholly their increase and arrival at this power' but he deemed it 'advisable to hinder their growth as much as can be.'" {215 Beer "Old Col." p.233}

William Harris wrote, in 1675, that the United Colonies had between 7000 and 8000 foot soldiers and about 650 horse-mounted.

"The U.S. Bureau of Census's closest estimate for New England Euranericans [whites] is pegged as of 1670 at a figure of 52,000."{216 Jennings p.30} Most of the English population was in what is now Massachusetts, Connecticut, and Rhode Island where the critical part of the war took place. Mass. Bay did take some small expeditions into what is now New Hampshire and Maine against the Indians there in 1675 &1676 and more there after the collapse of the southern tribes.

Man wrote "Sixteenth-century New England was home to 100,000 native people or more, a figure that was slowly increasing." {217 Man-Smithsonian Mag. Dec. 2005 p.99}

Malone wrote "It seems likely that over 75,000 Indians lived in what is now New England at the beginning of the 17ᵗʰ century". {218 Malone p.8}

The population of the natives in New England is said to have suffered a great decrease from the time of the arrival of the European diseases in the first decades of the 17th Century. As much as 90% died in certain villages, especially in the south. Some recovery probably had occurred by 1675.

There must have been many more Indian villages in colonial times than were ever noted by colonial writers and even more in pre-colonial / pre-plague years. Roger Williams wrote "...one would meet a dozen of their towns in the course of twenty miles..."{219 Fuller p.4-6} That reference would be to the Narragansett country. I have noted but nine village names of the Narragansetts, far fewer than William's note of "a dozen in twenty miles of travel".

Bradford wrote- "So the second of July [1621] they sent Mr. Edward Winslow and Mr. [Steven] Hopkins, with...Squanto for their guide" towards Massasoit's village of Pokanoket (Sowams/Montaup/Mt. Hope). {220 Bradford p.96} In their journey they followed the banks of the Nemasket and Titicut (Taunton) rivers, and, about those rivers one unidentified writer in "Mourt's Relation" (probably E. Winslow) notes "...upon it are and have been many towns, it being a good length. The ground is very good on both sides it being for the most part cleared. Thousands of men have lived there, which died in a great plague not long since; and pity it was and is to see so many goodly fields, and so well seated, without men to dress and manure the same...As we passed along we observed that there were few places by the river but had been inhabited, by reason whereof much ground was clear save [except] of weeds...Here let me not forget the valor and courage of some of the savages on the opposite side of the river, for there were remaining alive only two men, both aged...These two spying [us]...ran...to meet us at the bank, where with shrill voices and great courage standing charged upon us with their bows they demanded what we were, supposing us to be enemies..." {221 "Mourt's Relation" p.63&64}

That account indicates the willingness of those villagers to hang on their village site and community despite the probable reduction by the plague to such a small number of men. When the party reached Massasoit and had spent time with him, in one discussion Massasoit "named at least thirty places [villages]..." and "that they were his and would be at peace with us [Plymouth]..." {222 Ibid p.66}

New England Indians probably formed new villages on numerous occasions in pre-plague times. They were capable of establishing new villages by break-off groups, perhaps clans, when a need for such action occurred. It has been noted that most islands off of the New England coast had Indian villages. Somoset, the first Indian to greet the Pilgrims in English was a sagamore from Monhegan Island, Maine. All of the Elizabeth Island chain seem to have had villages upon them. Even remote Noman's Land Island was used regularly by one tribe of Capawack (Martha's Vineyard) and may have had year-round Indians at times. According to tribal stories the island belonged at one time to Tequenoman, a sachem at one time of Capawack, hence the name "Noman's Land Island" {223 Wood p.4}. Nantucket had five native villages in colonial times.

Floyd writes "Through New England, the total native American population had fallen to about 12,000 by the last quarter of the 17th century."{224 Floyd p.9} Losses in King Philip's War, natives sent into slavery and hundreds fleeing north and west could account for such a decrease.

The population of Indians in present New England in 1675 could be guessed at somewhere between 30,000 and 60,000 the majority were in southern New England. About a quarter of any population can be said to be able -bodied men capable of combat. The actual number of Indian combatants against the English in the southern parts is the significant figure for consideration and not a quarter of the total Indian population. At the start of the war the total populations of the English and of the Indians in New England were probably close in number, but whereas almost all Englishmen in New England were at the very least against the native insurrection, the natives were of many different inclinations. Some of those were:

1. Those who wanted to strike-out against the English and readily joined fully in the war;
2. Those who had animosity to the English and engaged in one or more assaults, quickly had second thoughts and tried to act peacefully or attempted to make peace, such as the Podunk of central Connecticut;
3. Those who stayed in place and out of the war until attacked or threatened such as some Nipmuck and most Narragansetts;
4. Those, such as Wonalecett and his people, who withdrew from the Merrimac valley in Massachusetts to kindred people near

present-day Concord New Hampshire or the Wabbaquassett of Connecticut who seemed to go into hiding;

5. Those, who in the last few months of the war, were prevailed upon to actually go into the field with the English against their fellow natives, such as some of the Cape Cod Wampanoag, some of the Massachusetts (most of the Massachusetts/Praying Indians had been confined on Deer Island) some Niantics, and even the Pequots the very people English writers had talked of exterminating;

6. Uncas' Mohegans who were fully English allies from the time of the Pequot War and on and

7. The Mohawks of New York, who made repeated incursions on the warring Indians after Dec.1675 when N.Y. Gov. Andros asked them to do so, but who never participated directly with the English.

The success the English had in manipulating Indians to fight for them is striking. Re-quoting Salisbury - "Charles II's commissioners after their visit to New England in 1664, charged that the missionaries were doing nothing for the natives except to undermine their traditional structure of authority." {225 Salisbury p.201} The missionaries deserve some of the credit or blame for that success.

The distrust of Indians that permeated English thinking caused the English to hold back from seeking help from uninvolved Indians during the early months. Later they became more confident that some Indians could be used. I suspect the loyal spying (disloyal to their own race and heritage) of several Praying Indians finally convinced the English leaders that the time for manipulation had come. Intimidation of some of the Cape Cod villages was certainly a factor in manipulation, and examples found of that were unapologetically noted in Plymouth Colony Records as follows;

" Att a meeting of the council of war for this jurisdiction held at Plymouth Aug. 4,1675…In reference vuto a company of natives now in custody, brought in to Plymouth, being men weomen, and children, in number (112) vpon seriouse and deliberate consideration and agitation concerning them, the conclusion is as followeth; that whereas, upon examination, it is found that seuerall of them haue bine actors in the late rising and warr…and the rest complyers with them therein, which they have done contrary to engagement and couenant made and plighted [complied?] with this colonie, which they haue pfidiously broken, [many, if not all of the Cape Cod tribes were stripped of their weapons and really forced to agree to loyalty to Plymouth and disloyalty to Philip.] as appeereth further alsoe in that they did not discouer that pnisious plott which Philip...completed against vs,... the councell adjudged them to be sold and deuoted vnto servitude, exceptimg some few of them...are to be disposed of...to make sale of them in the countryes behalfe." {226 Shurtleff p.173} And a second record "The councel of warr for this jurisdiction, being ...the second of Sept.1675, to consider of a ceraine psell of Indians lately come into Sandwich in a submissiue way...do find that they are in the same condition of rebellion as those formerly condemmed to seruitude... that the said Indians being in number fifty seauen, are condemed to ppetuall servitude...to make sale of them, for and to the vse of the colonie... ."{227 Shurtleff p.174}

Sandwich is a town on Cape Cod. None of the Wampanoag villages on the Cape seem to have helped the hostiles. Those villages were near to Plymouth and were affected by missionary efforts and intimidation. These acts by Plymouth, in modern legal definition, were "crimes against humanity," and, in any age, they were crimes against humanity in the eye of man's creator. It was also an obscene way to fund a war, albeit an effective way to coerce Indian villages to cooperate.

Could not or would not one Christian of this colonial society voice the words of Matthew 25 strongly enough to appear in the record at that time- the spoken words of Christ that Matthew made written: "as you do unto these my least brethren you do unto me." Well, perhaps Elliot did.

Even in the Irish rebellion of 1641-1652 many Irish-born took part with the English-Scotch forces against the native rebels. Native-born Irish were sometimes leaders of suppression forces.{228 Emmet}

If all the natives of New England had chosen to make a concerted, resolute, persistent effort to drive the English out of the country or force them into small submissive enclaves, they surely would have been able to succeed. The addition of help for the colonists from outside the region would have made it more difficult for the natives. How much of such help would be needed to maintain an English presence or obtain a defeat of the natives is another question. The English of New York were not that strong at that time, and concern for their own survival against the possibility of a local native uprising would probably keep them at home. Direct physical help from the mother country might have occurred at some point, however, the Puritan Colonies were in disfavor with the home government. England might have intentionally held off physical aid for some time in order to weaken those colonies and that aid could have easily arrive, if at all, too late to save those colonies. Some English leaders outside of New England were unfriendly toward New England. Lord Vaughan, Governor of Jamaica in 1675 suggested to the Committee for Trade & Plantations, that it might be good time for the King to take action against Mass. Bay for its' non-compliance with trade laws, Vaughan noted "the Indians [there] being in rebellion…and not likely to be reduced". Actually, in Oct. 1676, 1300 regular troops were prepared in England and arrived in Virginia in Jan. 1677 to put down Bacon's Rebellion. So disaffected was the English government toward Mass. Bay that the use of the same troops sent to Virginia was considered for Mass. Bay after Virginia in order to coerce that colony to better behavior. It is doubtful that Red Coats, without the guidance of some savvy colonists or lackey Indians would have much success against Indian methods, and the more successful the patriotic Indian effort, the less likely there would be any lackey Indians, Also, colonist guides could be specially targeted by snipers. Bacon had stated; "may not 500 Virginians beat them [2000 Red Coats], we having the same advantages against them, which the Indians have against us."{230 Webb p.80} Unlike New England, Virginia was a Crown colony, so it could be controlled. Its governor served at the King's discretion, and the governor Berkeley was recalled in Feb. 1677 well after the rebellion was put down. Thus assistance for New England was not the same as assistance for Virginia.

Edward Randolph, one of the Royal Commissioners, had been directed to investigate the political situation in Mass. Bay in March 1676. His report, delivered Oct.12, 1676, suggested "…that 3 frigates of 40 guns with 3 ketches well maned lying a League or two below Boston … would bring them all to his Mat.'s own terms and doe more in one Weeks time than all of the Orders of King and Council to them in Seven years…".{231 Webb p.237} On Oct. 20, 1676, royal orders were set out that after the situation in Virginia was settled, the fleet and troops at Virginia were to proceed to Boston and to enforce the King's pleasure. That plan failed to occur due to delays in Virginia. Of course many factors would be different if the Indians had appeared to be clearly winning a war against the New Englanders at that time.

The English government's displeasure with Mass. Bay goes back to years before 1676. Beer wrote-"In 1635, legal proceedings were also instituted against the patentees of the Massachusetts Charter. In order to enable the Crown to resume it's authority in this region, the New England Council at the same time resigned its' patent. Finally after two years, the quo warranto suit was decided in favor of the Crown, and Charles I declared that he had taken the whole management of New England into his hands...he appointed Sir Fernando Gorges as governor. For technical reasons this legal victory was ineffective, and before other measures could be adopted, the political situation in England became acute...momentous issues brought to a head by...the Long Parliament" {232 Beer "Origin" p.329}. Next came the rise of the Puritans and the English Civil war. Only after five decades later in the fall of 1684, was the charter of Massachusetts annulled. The weakness of New England at that time due to King Philip's War is considered a factor in that charter loss.

In 1685, Charles II died and was succeeded by his brother the Duke of York, who became King James II. James created the dominion of New England which included the New England colonies, New York and New Jersey in 1685. In 1686 he appointed Sir Edmond Andros to head the dominion, disempowering the Puritan government of Mass. Bay, the probable main purpose for the creating the dominion. Fortunately for the Puritans, James' daughter and her husband William of Orange, took on the purposes of the opposition and invaded England from the Netherlands in Nov. of 1687. James was injecting Roman Catholicism into Protestant England. James was forced to flee to France and William and Mary became joint rulers of Great Britain. When Boston became aware of the new Protestant rulers, some of its former leaders arrested Andros and reappointed the former governor. The new King and Queen went along with the dissolution of the dominion, but the independence of Mass. Bay was never quite the same until after the revolution of a century later.

A large and persistent assistance by the Hodosonee (Five Nations/ Iroquois) to the Puritan colonies would seem to have been the only way to overcome a full, concerted, persistent effort by the New England natives to overcome the English. There probably was nothing in the traditions of the New England tribes that could make them conceive of such a complete combination or union, but even something less might have achieved victory if only other New England Indians and the Hodosonee had refrained from assisting the colonists.

The above speculation on what could have happened in 1675 is useful if only to try to debunk the history that says the colonists defeated the Indians in a valiant effort by a superior society with an inevitable result. Actually, it was those Indians who assisted the English in combat, in guidance, in gathering of intelligence, and in the possible persuasion of hostiles to surrender, that caused the hostiles' defeat.

The status of the war in the early spring of 1676 appeared to be going unfavorably for the English. Even though it was only a fraction of the total body of Indians who were warring, they seemed to be winning. The attacks on settlements were usually surprises, and widespread movements by small numbers of English were extremely dangerous and thereby, seemingly rare. Neither Indians nor English could plant their crops. New England, before the war, had crops that they exported for cash. During the war, they were forced to buy or seek charity to help their food stocks. A ship full of food supplies even arrived from Ireland.

The numerical superiority of English manpower was greatly diminished by the need to keep enough men in arms in each town to guard against unpredictable attack. The unpredictability and frequency of random attacks was as effective as a great strategy by the Indians, but a study of the attacks appears rather to be spontaneous efforts made by many different groups of Indians of various sizes (the attack on Clark's garrison near Plymouth was by eleven Indians), motivated by a general animosity toward the English and not by any central planning or leadership.

There are many figures given, by contemporaries, as to the numbers of hostile Indians; only occasionally does one seem reasonably accurate. Such a figure, as the one given by a friendly Indian to the English, was that Philip had 250 men with him at Nipsachuck. At that time, he had with him his own Pokanokets, the Pocassets, possibly the Sekonnets, Assonets and or the Seekonks. The first three had, just days before, escaped English entrapment at Pocasset swamp. Probably no village in New England had more than 150 warriors and most less. Villages with small populations probably avoided involvement in the war. The first three villages mentioned were noted in records and were on the larger size. The Pokanoket village of Montaup/Sowams probably was the largest of all the Wampanoag villages. I believe the figure of 250 for the three fits well. It is well to note that by this that when Philip launched or was launched into war, he had the probable commitment of only 100 to 150 of his own Pokanoket warriors. George Memecho was a Praying Indian (a Natick) who guided Capt. Wheeler when he was ambushed near Brookfield in July 1675. He was captured there, later escaping and providing the English with intelligence about Philip- "Upon Fri. Aug. 5 Philip and his company came to us [Memecho would have been with Nipmuck hostiles then] ...six miles from a swamp where they killed our men [Wheeler's men]. Philip brought with him about 48 men..." Only 48 men in his company then! {233 Drake B.of I. III p.29-30} That would have been near the Nipmuck village of Quabaug.

At this time, the will and confidence of the colonists in the outly-ing towns must have been low while the confidence of the leadership in secure Boston, Hartford and Plymouth was still robust. An appraisal of the state of affairs applicable to that time, although composed after events turned, appears in "N.S."'s narrative dated and sent to London July 22,1676- "The Dispensation we lay under was Cloudy and Af-frightening, Fresh Messengers (like Job's Servants) hourly arriving to bring the Doleful Tidings of New Massacres, Slaughters and Devas-tations committed by the Brutish Heathens; and certainly it cannot but deserve both Wonder and Commiseration, that these parts which were not many Moneths since hardly to be Parrallele'd for Plenty and Security, are now almost destroyed and laid Waste by the Cruelties of a Bloody (and sometimes Despicable) Enemy; who are now so well furnished with Arms and Ammunition (by the base Treachery we fear of some of our Neighbors) [New Yorkers, Dutch?] so instructed in Discipline by Experience, and heightened in Pride by Successe, That unless our God (whose tender Mercies are over all his Works) in Com-passion to the English Nation in this Wilderness, wonderfully appear for our Deliverance, Nothing could be expected but an utter Desolation;...".{234 Saltonstall p.78} This appraisal is exaggerated somewhat to garner sympathy and to enhance the idea of God's rescue as it does further on in his narrative by later events. However many of the colonists did then feel desperation.

There would be a change in events that lead from the apex of the Indian success to their decline and utter defeat. Mary's time of redemption could almost be seen as the time of the war's turning point. Also making Mary Rowlandson central to the war's history was her witnessing of the radical change noticed in the warrior's mood and temper after the attack on Sudbury April 18, 1676 compared to what it was before the attack. This may have been perceived as an omen as described by her earlier.

Chapter Twenty-Nine

◆

Redemption

On May 2nd or 5th, Mary, Mr. Hoar and the two Praying Indians set off in freedom. Just before leaving, Mary noted; "But to my going home, where it may seem a remarkable change of Providence : At first they were all against it, except my husband would come for me; but afterwards they assented to it, and seemed much to rejoyce in, some askt me to send them some Bread, others some Tobacco, others shaking me by the hand, ...not one moving a hand or a tongue against it...[I] have been in the midst of those roaring Lyons, and Savage Bears, that feared neither God, or Man, nor the Devil, by night and day, alone and in company: sleeping all sorts together, and yet not one of them ever offered me the least abuse of unchastity to me, in word or action. Though some [of her fellow Christians] are ready to say, I speak it for my own credit; But I speak it in the presence of God, and to his Glory". It must be emphasized here what it would seem a society can teach it members- no Indian seems to hate the English woman; no Indian commits the slightest "unchastity" towards her. Mary needed to assert she had not been violated when it was known that Europeans expected such, and how her particular colonial society often told of the natives "filthy lusts", would have created such a need.

English narrators were not apt to tell of Englishmen raping Indian women, but Gookin does tell of the murder of three Indian women and three children, and it sounds as if rape might have also occurred.

"About the ninth of Aug...[1676] about four miles from Watertown mill..." eleven or twelve English came upon "two squaws, wifes to two of our Indian soldiers...and one young woman and three children whereof one was a nursing infant...[and] one Indian man with them...

they disarmed him...for he was newly come in from our army, and had not delivered his arms..." Next, they threatened to kill him but relented and sent him back to his Praying town but without the women who were then picking berries. "the English came to them and sat down, and smok'd it [pipe?] where they were and exchanged with them bread and cheese for hurtleberries, and then the English left [them], but not being [gone] a mile, four of the English went back to the squaws [then took them to] a secret place, and there murdered them all and stript such as had coats on."{235 Gookin "Sufferings" p.513} Gookin's manuscript, "...Sufferings..." was not published at that time, but the manuscript was discovered in 1836 by antiquarians and later published. Such stories as this may be why it was not released then. Gookin was giving information of murder of neutrals or allies and suspicion (at least, mine) of rape. Without mentioning rape, Gookin was clearly offended that any of this could be done to any of his Praying Indians. Murder is worse than rape, but rape and murder such as these are known to have occurred in wars, but seldom acknowledged by the offending side. The Indian side had no way to record such crimes. While English writers accused "savages" of such crimes and noted none by their own, the reports of the English captives in the east always denied rape.

All the other English captives taken in King Philip's War and later released probably felt the same joy as did Mary. In other times in other Indian wars where captives were held longer and in relatively stable locations, many captives refused or declined to depart from the Indians. Mary Jamison's story, dwelt on earlier, is an excellent example of why captives chose to remain with associates of their captors or captors themselves, that because those Indians evolved into their friends and or because they preferred the new life better than their former. It is true that many captives taken in various parts were horribly treated at first. Mutilations and tortures even to death were common, but even those who survived such treatments were gradually accepted as equals into Indian life. Drake wrote- "The daughter of Mrs. [Ann] Hutchinson, eight years old...carried into captivity [when Ann was killed in a raid by a Hudson River tribe in Sept. 1643] remained a prisoner for four years, when she was delivered to the Dutch governor...who restored her to her friends. She had forgotten her native language [English] and was unwilling to be taken from the Indians."{236 Drake "B of I" p.69}

Eunice Williams captured in 1704 from Deerfield, daughter of Rev. John Williams, was adopted by the Caughnawaga/Mohawks (Roman Catholic Mohawks who had separated from the other Mohawks) and married one of them. She refused repeated and persistent attempts to repatriate her, even when she returned to New England for visits to her family. {237 Baker p.153&154}

Abigail Nims, four years of age when captured in 1704 with her mother from Deerfield, was also adopted by the Caughnawaga. In 1714, her captor brought her to Westfield, Mass. and there received twenty -five pounds for her. By 1715, she fled back to Canada and, the same year married, one Josiah Rising, another New England captive who also would not return. {238 Baker P.235, 237, 246 & 247}

Drimmer gives a quote from one Colonel. Henry Bouquet who was involved during Pontiac's War and led an army against the Ohio Indians in1764- "But it must not be denied that there were even some grown persons [American captives released]...who showed an unwillingness to return. The Shawanese were obliged to bind several of their [exchangeable] prisoners and force them along to the camp, and some women, who had been delivered up, afterwards found means to escape and run back to the Indian towns. Some who could not make their escape, clung to their savage acquaintances at parting, and continued many days in bitter lamentations, even refusing sustenance."{239 Drimmer p.14}

Ben Franklin, in a letter to a friend in England in 1753, wrote - "When a white person of either sex have been taken prisoner, young by the Indians, and have a while lived among them, tho' ransomed by their Friends, and treated with all imaginable tenderness to prevail with them to stay...yet in a Short time become discussed with our manner of life, and the care and pains necessary to support it, and take the first good opportunity of escaping into the Woods, from whence there is no reclaiming them. When an Indian child has been brought up among us, taught our language and habituated to our Customs, yet if he goes to see his relations and makes one Indian ramble with them, there is no persuading him ever to return." Franklin went on further to theorize why this occurred - mankind left the tribal hunter-gather lifestyle not out of preference, but out of necessity brought about by crowding or by compulsion by a powerful outside society.{240 Kolodny-N.Y. Times Mag.1-31-93}

We see that the heavily populated areas of precolonial Central and South America as well as many old world societies, were nontribal. Tenochtitlan (now Mexico City), the highly structured urban capital of the Aztec empire, had an estimated population of 300,000 circa 1450. London's population was then about 120,000.{241 Brandon p.69} The Europeans and likely the Aztec considered themselves superior to neighboring societies, especially neighboring tribal societies. Yet, would many individuals from urbanized societies, European or Aztec immersed forcibly or accidentally into tribal life for a period of five or six years choose to leave such a life?

Repeating William Penn who said of the Indians- "We sweat, and toil to live, their pleasure feeds them, I mean, their Hunting, Fishing and Fouling. In this they are sufficiently revenged on us." Well, not sufficiently, but the point he seems to make is that they had a more satisfying life.

In Massachusetts, laws were passed to punish any English found to be living with the Indians because this happened occasionally. Connecticut passed a law providing at least three years imprisonment plus a fine or corporal punishment for any white found living with Indians. That law followed the case of one William Baker living with the Indians. {242 Salisbury "Conquest" p.114} Baker was whipped in 1637 by Plymouth and punished in Connecticut for "uncleanliness", having lived with a squaw there in Connecticut. {243 Bartlett p.66}

Mary, Mr. Hoar, Nepanet (called Tom Dublet) and Tatatiquinea (called Peter Conway) set off for Boston, passing through the abandoned Lancaster where Mary noted not "one house left standing." They stayed in an apparently abandoned farm house, probably on the road to Marlborough, that was "yet standing." Lancaster was later resettled but again attacked on Sept.11,1697. Before noon they reached Concord which had only small damage from the Indians. From Concord, they continued on to Boston "where I [Mary] met my dear Husband, but the thoughts of our dear Children, one being dead, and the other we could not tell where, abated our comfort each to other. I was not before so much hem'd in with the merciless and cruel Heathen, but now with pittiful, tender hearted and compassionate Christians. In that poor, and distressed and beggardly condition I was received in, I was kindly entertained in several Houses: so much love I received from several (some of whom I knew, and others I knew not) that I and not capable to declare it." Perhaps if the natives could have kept the pressure on longer, Mary and all the other "distressed Christians" of New England might have considered seeking "much love" and to "be kindly entertained" back where they had come from, England.

"The twenty pounds, the price of my redemption was raised by some Boston Gentlemen, And Mrs. Usher..." . The government of Mass. Bay avoided this ransom and was spared the use of some the money derived from their sale of surrendered Indians.

The overall treatment Mary received while being held captive was mild; the "Heathen" were not "merciless and cruel" to her. She suffered the horror of the attack and the viewing of the slaughter of some relatives and neighbors. She suffered many of the discomforts of movements through the wilds in winter weather and the meager nourishments, as did the natives she was with. Those Indians of her gender and age were probably better physiologically able than Mary to cope, but there were many aged and many young children among them who were stressed more than Mary. Mary suffered the loss of her six year old from the wounding by the Indians, but how many Narragansetts, young and old were killed by the English assaults in December? She suffered the loss of friends and associates for at least eighty-one days. She was not moved from New England to another remote land to labor in slavery for the rest of her life as were hundreds of the natives. It is a credit to Mary that she had the initiative and courage to go from wigwam to wigwam seeking nourishment, but it is also to the credit of the Indians that she always managed to get something, even if she was rejected by some at times before receiving from others. Also, it needs to be considered that all those natives of wigwams other than her own had no reason other than compassion or charity to share with the begging English captive any of their meager supplies, gathered mostly by their own efforts.

It was June 29th when Mary and her husband, traveling eastward, came across Rev. William Hubbard "who told us that our Son Joseph was come into Major Waldrens... [and also] my Sister's son".

I have considered Hubbard as the possible writer of Mary's narrative based on his personal association with the Rowlandsons and the similarities of style and rhetoric in Mary's and his own history. A verbatim description of the chaste treatment Mary experienced appeared both in Hubbard's history of 1677 and Mary's narrative published five years later. If he were the writer of both however, it is remarkable that he seemed to be such a fabricator in his own history while so many frank statements of Mary's are passed on, seemingly uncensored.

Just one day later someone came to Rev. Rowlandson and informed him "that his Daughter was come in at Providence...Her coming in was after this manner: She was traveling one day with the Indians [these would be likely Narragansetts and Wampanogs exiting the Nipmuck country, leaving their alliance with the Nipmuck and thereby collapsing their resistance effort], with her basket at her back; the company of Indians were got before her, and gone out of sight, all except one Squaw; she followed the Squaw till night, and then both of them lay down, having nothing over them but the heavens, and under them but the earth. Thus she traveled three days together, not knowing whither she was going: having nothing to eat or drink but water, and Green Hirtle-berries. At last they came into Providence, where she was kindly entertained by several of that Town."

We can and should speculate of the squaw who led Mary's daughter to freedom. One theory would be that the squaw took an opportunity to secure from the English some individual advantage due to her bringing in the child herself. The narrative gives no further information about the squaw. Wouldn't the writer gladly tell if that was the squaw's motive? It would be unlikely that a squaw would leave her tribe or clan seeking acceptance by the English. A more likely explanation would be that the captors saw the futility of holding the girl or even the use of English ransom any longer and, out of kindness allowed one adult squaw, who knew the way to Providence, to take the child and there leave her. A squaw, if careful, could return to her people without letting those of the town follow her.

Soon, the ten year old Mary was returned to her family, Mary senior noted - "Thus hath the Lord brought me and mine out of that horrible pit, and hath set us up in the midst of tender-hearted and compassionate Christians." Young Mary's release occurred near the end of June just at the time the Narragansetts and the Wampanoags were departing from their former Nipmuck allies and likely heading in a south, south-easterly direction but more easterly from Providence.

Earlier, several letters had been sent by some Nipmucks (probably at the suggestion of some Praying Indians) attempting to placate Mass. Bay authorities towards them in particular. One letter, signed by "Sam Sachem" and "Written by Simon Boshokum Scribe," had this in part "...Philip and Quanipin went away into their Country againe, and I know they were much afraid, because of our offer to join with the English, and therefore they went back into their own Country, and I know they will make no Warre; therefore because some English men came to us, Philip and Quanapum sent to kill them, but I said, if any kill them, I'll kill them."{244 Drake "Book of I" p.84} A shameful way to try to gain an accommodation with your war time opponent.

It may be that the Narragansett and Wampanoag would not bargain any more with Mass. Bay or the Nipmucks, but would allow young Mary's release at Providence.

Nine months later in March 1677, another ten year old child would experience effects from captivity, this time it would be an Indian boy, the same boy Mary Rowlandson had knitted a cap for at the request of his father, Philip. John Cotton wrote in a letter to I. Mather - "Today Philip's son went to be sold as a slave." [245 Burke, prologue] He, along with his mother, had been captured in July 1676. His sale occurred only after considerable debate as to whether he should be executed instead. Such talk of execution probably was not to be vindictive; rather, it probably was due to the apprehension in the European mentality that some future insurrection would be able to rally around Philip's natural successor if the child were kept alive in New England, even as a slave.

Chapter Thirty

✦

The Collapse

After the Narragansetts and the Wampannoags departed from the Nipnucks and their country, more attacks then occurred in Plymouth colony. These appeared just as poorly coordinated and planned as the previous attacks throughout the greater New England area had been. But now, knowing of the break-up of the Indian confederacy, the English gained tremendously in confidence. The emphasis shifted toward search and destroy missions with less concern for the defense of each settlement. The average English soldier could now feel far more confident of his safety. Most of the English soldiers were farmers or tradesmen, but many of the older men, probably officers, had served in Cromwell's army where "wholesale slaughter of the Irish and his selling of many into West Indian slavery parallels exactly the policy adopted by the American Puritans in King Philip's War two decades later". {246 Slotkins p.42}

The hostile groups of Indians did a pitiful job of protecting themselves. Everywhere, it seems, small parties of Indians were surprised while food gathering, by English troops who were very often accompanied by Indian allies. Many times traitors led English to small Indian parties that never seemed to have any plan of defense. Hundreds of Indians fell to easy capture leading to exported enslavement, involuntary servitude in colonial towns, or executions. Yet, groups of hostiles continued making small sporadic attacks in Plymouth Colony, Rhode Island and in the Connecticut River valley.

The Indians who lived north of the Merrimac never collapsed and continued warring on and off against a much smaller English population for decades, and many of the southern hostiles joined them after August 1676.

> I. Mather noted on June 30th "...an Indian was come into Rehoboth, who informed that Philip was not far off, and that he had but thirty men (besides women and children) with him...he said recently the Mauquawogs [Mohawks] had killed fifty of his men." {247 I. Mather p.128}

Philip never becoming the great leader needed, still attempted "with all the forces he could get," a significant attack on Taunton on July 11,1676. The town was well prepared with defending soldiers having been forewarned by a Negro slave who had escaped from Indian capture "a little before". The attackers withdrew after only burning two houses. Imagine, a slave helping his enslavers!

Mather wrote "July 8. Whereas the Council at Boston had lately emitted a Declaration, signifying, that such Indians as did within 14 days come in to the English, might hope for mercy…"{247b Ibid p.128}. Many Indians may have fallen for this vague offer not recognizing how dangerous it could be to them. A proclamation by the Mass. Council on Sept. 16th, 1676 (by which time the greater number of the hostiles had surrendered or been captured) stated Mass. Bay's intentions more honestly than the July proclamation – "such of them [captives] as shall appear to have imbued their hands in English blood should suffer death here…" "Here", in this case, meant New England rather than being shipped out of the country into slavery {247c Shurtleff Mass. Records V 115}.

Throughout July and August many of the sachems were either killed in fighting or executed after capture. Even their attempt at peace did not save the Nipmuck sachems from executions on the Boston Commons.

"In June, 1676, when in the woods about twenty miles above Piscataqua [York, Maine] his [Pessacus's] party was ambushed by the Mohawk Indians." Pessacus was there killed by the Mohawks. Chapin says Pessacus had succeeded his brother Miantonmi as chief sachem of the Narragansetts. If so, it would appear he relinquished that role at some time to his nephew, Canonchet. Quanapin was another nephew of Pessacus. {248 Chapin p.86&54}

Akkompoin, Philip's uncle and counselor, was killed on July 31ˢᵗ as he was crossing the Titicut river on a "great tree" which the Indians had felled across the river.{249 Hubbard p.261} The next day, Captain Church's party returned to that site and spotted an Indian sitting on the same tree, Church prepared to fire upon that Indian when a lackey with him "called hastily to him, not to fire, for he believed it was one of their own men. Upon which the Indian upon the stump, looked about, and Capt. Church's Indian seeing his face, perceived his mistake, for he knew him to be Philip...Philip...leaped down on the other side of the river and made his escape." {250 Church p.110} Was Philip there on the site of his uncle's death, alone, lamenting the loss of perhaps a beloved adviser?

That same day (July 31), Church captured Philip's wife and son and received information that "Quanapin and the Narragansetts" were drawing off toward their own country.{251 Church p.103} It seems likely that Quanapin and Weetamoe parted company at about that time. It appeared, from the histories, that the Indian groups were splitting off from one another and becoming small vulnerable groups. The need for sustenance and the lack of leadership and direction probably caused such unwise actions.

On Aug. 6ᵗʰ a turncoat Indian informed the people of Taunton that he would lead them to some Indians, whereupon soldiers went with him and captured 36 Indians. For an individual hostile Indian to approach the English with intelligence worthwhile to them, he would have to have had the expectation that he would be granted at least his present and future liberty. It is reasonable to suspect that such expectation was engendered by the English or their lackeys. From that group of Indians, Weetamoe "escaped alone". Not long after that day, some of those English from Taunton came across the body of a squaw on the Shawomet shore of the Titicut river (Somerset, Ma.). They cut off the woman's head and brought it back to Taunton where it was set up on a pole for display. The Indian prisoners, there seeing the head, "made a most horrid and diabolical Lamentation crying out it was their Queen's head". {252 I. Mather p.137}

According to Church, five days later, an Indian appeared on the land across from the landing place of Trip's ferry on Aquidneck Island. He was near the end of that neck of land that held Montaup/Mt. Hope called Consumpsit. The Indian signaled the English on Aquidneck to fetch him over. When he landed, he informed the English that he could direct them to Philip and "seven" men with him on "Mounthope Neck." Per Church - "...he reported that he was fled from Philip who [said he] has killed my brother [Mather says only "an Indian" was killed by Philip] just before I came away, for giving some advise that displeased him. And said he was fled for fear of meeting with the same his brother had met with." {253 Church p.121} Those English at the landing sent for Ben Church who was then visiting his wife where they were living on the island. Church hastened to Trip's where he interviewed "the deserter". {254 Mather p.138} & {254 Church p.121} The next day would be Philip's last.

Most readers of Thomas Church's narrative probably do not notice how he presents this "deserter" as a strange, previously unknown Indian to those English and Ben Church. Thomas refers to him variously as; "an Indian", "the deserter", " a fellow of good sense." He would also seem to be referred to as "pilot", the Indian assigned to Capt. Golding as his aide in the ambush at Mt. Hope.{255 Church p.120-125} In English word usage then, pilot and guide meant the same. I suspect this informer was "Alderman" an Indian so-named by the English and well known to Ben Church. The informer had "offered Capt. Church, to pilot him to Philip". Church offered "Capt. Golding the honor to beat up Philip's headquarters. He accepted the offer and had his allotted number drawn out to him, and the pilot." T. Church does not say that it was Golding and his pilot who shot Philip, nor does he identify the actual shooter by name at first but allows that to be obscured by writing- "The man that shot down Philip, ran with all speed to Capt. Church, and informed him of his exploit." {256 Church p.121-125} Two paragraphs further on, Thomas wrote; "Philip having one very remarkable hand, being much scarred, occasioned by the splitting of a pistol in it formerly, Capt. Church gave the head and that hand [of Philip] to Alderman, the Indian who shot him, to show such gentlemen as would bestow gratuities upon him; and accordingly he got many a penny by it."{257 Church p.126} Richard Hutchinson,, who wrote extensively about the war ,(his account published in 1677) and of the events at Mt. Hope on Aug. 12[th,] wrote; "...the Indian Guide and the Plimouth Man being together, the guide espied an Indian and bids the Plimouth-man shoot, whose Gun went not off...with that the Indian looked about, and was going to shoot, but the Plimouth-man prevented him , and shot the Enemy through the Body, dead...upon Search, it appeared to be King Philip..."{258 R. Hutchinson p.105}. Although Hutchinson applied the credit for the killing to the Englishman, he does specify the "guide" as being the second person involved and his story otherwise sounds just like T. Church's, except that Thomas avoids specifying the "guide" as the killer. The link between "the deserter", "the pilot" or "guide" and Alderman is avoided. Why would Thomas present the identity of the deserter/informer as unknown if that Indian was Alderman? Much earlier in his narrative, he wrote that, early in July 1675; "Mr. Church then returned to the island [Aquidneck] to seek provisions for the army [there he] meets with Alderman, a noted Indian, that was just come over from the squaw Sachem's cape of Pocasset having deserted from her and brought over his family, who gave him [Ben] an account of the Indians, and where each of the Sagamore's headquarters was."{259 Church p.47} Alderman was a Pocasset and at that time, the Pocassets had escaped from the Pocasset swamp with Philip so Alderman was a deserter as of then.

I. Mather in his "Brief History...", released just days after Philip's death, wrote that Philip's killer was "Alderman" who belonged to Weetamoe's village and at the beginning of the war he had gone to the governor of Plymouth "manifesting his desire to be at peace with the English and immediately withdrew to an Island [Aquidneck?] not having ingaged against the English nor for them, before this time."{260 I. Mather p.138} William Harris wrote "He (Philip) was shot through the heart by an Indian who lives on Aquidneck Island... . {260b Harris p.85}

Perhaps Thomas or his father realized that an informed reader might not believe that the Indian who decided at the very beginning of the war to desert his own village and seek acceptance from the English would then appear back (with family) with the hostiles when the war effort was almost expired. But that Philip was such a desperate, nasty savage that he would kill any follower who suggested peace is such a good story that it needed to so be presented, but such a story might be suspect if the record of the Indian Alderman in the center of that story was known. Church's account was published forty years after the death of Philip, so the story of Alderman being both the killer and the brother of an Indian allegedly slain by Philip would have then been widely known. One possible reason for keeping Alderman obscure in a work published in 1716 is that Thomas may have simply copied from his father's notes of 1676. It is typical, however, of the creative, embellished versions of events as presented by Mather, Hubbard, Church and some other colonial writers.

Mather added a little more to the stories of Philip's last days. - "That very night [Aug. 11] Philip had been dreaming that he was fallen into the Hands of the English; and now just as he was telling his Dream with Advise unto Friends to fly for their Lives, lest the Knave who had newly gone from them , should shew the English how to come at them, Church... fell upon them."{261 Mather p.139} But where would such a story come from? Church does not claim to have captured any Indian on Aug. 12th or any Indians until Aug. 28th, and no captives are reported in the area before Mather's release of his Narrative on about Aug. 21st.

Church's description of Philip's death is about as degrading as anyone could imagine; "Capt. Church knowing it was Philip's custom, to be foremost in the flight...[he] ran directly on two of Capt. Church's ambush...the Englishman's gun missing fire, he bid the Indian fire away... [he] sent one musket bullet through his heart and another not two inches from it. [Note this paragraph is almost the same as Hutchinson's but Church does not identify the Indian shooter.] He fell upon his face in the mud and water with his gun under him...Capt. Church ordered his body to be pulled out of the mire to the upland. So some of Capt. Church's Indians took hold of him by his stockings, and some by his small breeches and drew him through the mud to the upland; and a doleful, great, naked, and dirty beast he looked like. Capt. Church then said, that foreasmuch as he had caused many Englishman's body to be unburied, and to rot above ground, that not one of his bones should be buried. And calling his old Indian executioner, bid him behead and quarter him." B.Church had that executioner saying as he prepared to do the deed- " he [Philip] had been a very great man, and had made many a man afraid of him, but so big as he was, he would now chop his arse for him." {262 Church p.120-125} T. Church wrote that the Capt. gave the head and hand to the killer but, for sure Philip's head did not stay with his killer, if indeed he ever had it, for it was stuck on a pole in a prominent place in Plymouth where it remained many years. It doesn't matter how much of Church's last three paragraphs, are accurate; what matters is that that is the way he wanted to describe Philip's desecration. It seems that Church, (father or son), saw a need to denigrate the protagonist of the war as much as he could. That need was to reassure the colonist that the fault of this terrible war was upon the Indian or at least some Indian leaders.

Ben Church was born in 1639; his narrative was written two years before his death in 1718. He noted "having my minutes by me, my son has taken care and pains to collect from them the ensuing narrative...which I have had the perusal of, and find nothing amiss..."{263 Church p. X}

So the main Indian protagonist comes to as inglorious end as Thomas can describe. Descendants of Philip's family can overcome some of the disgrace that description might cause them if they consider what happened to a king and a lord protector in England in the same era. On the 27th of January 1649, King Charles I was sentenced to death as a "Tyrant, Traitor, Murderer and a public enemy of this nation." He was beheaded on January 30th, 1649. Then, after the Restoration in 1660, "The bodies of [some of the leaders of the Commonwealth] Cromwell, Ireton, Bradshaw were removed from [graves at] Westminster Abbey and hanged at Tyburn before burial in a common pit." Further, Cromwell's body "was exhumed, dragged to Tyburn and beheaded. His head was stuck on a pole outside of Westminster Hall where it remained for more than twenty years." {264 Cannon p.385}

Thomas Church, on his own or with his father's guidance, attempted to present the hostile Indians as cowardly, disloyal to their own people, terrible marksmen and never clever. However, any Indian who became an associate of his father was a favorable exception or somehow gained skill and virtue, and thereby, those were resolute, brave, clever, loyal and excellent marksmen.

According to some colonial writers, lackey Indians do all the menial work and all the dissecting of slain enemies whenever they are available; however, the English can perform the gruesome tasks when none are available.

On the basis of the available evidence, Philip could be and probably should be honored for what he seems to have tried to do for his people.

The evident attempt to seek as many natives as possible to join in war against the English, whether his own plan or from unnamed advisors, was the only way the natives could win and keep their way of life. It is also evident that Philip and his counselors should have known that a firm and sustainable union would be difficult to obtain. Each native village seemed always to hold their independence as their priority. Perhaps a better man than Philip could have convinced more natives to follow him as long as was needed, but where was that better man. How many years were there left before the time arrived when even a perfect leader could not dislodge the ever growing European population?

On August 16th, Quanapin surrendered himself and a band of natives in Rhode Island. He was taken to Newport where he was tried and found guilty along with his brothers Ashamattan and Sunkeejunasuc. It is written that he had admitted he fought the English at the Narragansett fort in Dec. 1675 and that he took part in the attack on Lancaster in Feb. 1676.{265 Chapin p.89} He was executed on Aug. 24th on the Newport Common.{266 LaFantasie} He may have acquired the role of "supreme" sachem after the execution of Canonchet.

Each village had its own sachem who ruled by inheritance and possibly also by gaining the approval of most of the villagers. If someone found they disliked their sachem, they could go and dwell elsewhere, it appears. It seems such movement was one of the individual's rights; of course, family ties might be the largest factor there.

Edward Winslow wrote- "Every sachem taketh care of the widow and the fatherless, also for such as are aged and any way maimed, if their friends be dead or unable to provide for them."

In the Algonquin societies here dealt with, the sachems came from a sort of "royal" linage, but the succession did not always follow the father to eldest son path. Some attention, it seems, was paid to capabilities in arriving at the determination of who would be the next sachem, and women were not ruled out. Weetamoe and Awashonks of the Wampanoag and Quaiapen and Weunquesh (daughter of Ninigret) of the Narragansett are examples of squaw sachems. A "supreme" sachem may have held some sway over the other village sachems of a tribal people such as the Narragansett, the Wampanoag, the Massachusett and the Pequot, but he or she was not supreme like a European king. Indeed this was a weakness of the Indian self-defense needs.

Quanapin seems to have been a cousin of Canonchet. His father was Cojonaquant, called by Williams a "poor beast (always drunk)", whose father was Mascus a younger brother of Canonicus (supreme sachem until his death in 1647). Mascus had four sons: Miantonomi, Yotaash, Pessacus and Cojonoquant. Canonicus had shared sachemship with Miantonomi until Miantonomi's execution in 1643. Pessacus may have assisted Canonicus as sachem after Miantonomi's execution. At some point in time, Miantonomi's son Canonchet became supreme sachem. Canonchet and Quanapin were first couisins, if the above is correct. {267 Chapin p.9, 53, 54, 61}

Quanapin was reported by one Capt. Moris to be "a lusty sachem and a very rogue..."{268 Drake B. of I p.53} "It appears that Quanopin had some difficulty with [some] Rhode Island people, who sometime before the war had cast him into prison, but by some means he had escaped and became active in the war." {269 Ibid p.53} "In 1672 Quanopin confirmed, by a writing, the sale of land previously granted by his father Coginaquan". { Ibid p.51} Cojonoquant's name appears as the seller of numerous plots and islands in Narragansett Bay. It is unbelievable that he would have had authority to sell any land. The English repeatedly picked whatever Indian might conveniently appear to possess some authority to put that Indian's name on a deed describing some land they desired.

Quanapin's admissions should not have justified his execution. The attack on the Narragansett country was aggression by the United Colonies, done even without the acknowledged permission of Rhode Island as required by the Royal charter of 1663 quoted earlier.

While there is no indication that Rhode Island attempted to excuse or grant permission for the invasion, they did nothing to prevent it or to make any known attempt to forewarn the Narragansetts of what was being planned. Rhode Island did, however, order the assistance of boats to transport some of the invaders to the Narragansett country. They did also contribute some supplies to that army, but that was after the army had entered that colony.

From the time of the United Colonies entrance into the colony followed by the first killing of natives and the destruction of native towns, Quanapin and the Narragansetts were justified in attacking any and all towns of the United Colonies.

From a letter sent to the Connecticut government by the Rhode Island assembly after the war's end and dated October 25, 1676, it is clear what the Rhode Island consensus was regarding the invasion of the Narragansetts . Connecticut, still lusting for control of lands in present southern Rhode Island, had moved into the area after the war. Rhode Island's letter seemed a threat to expose the injustice of the United Colonies attack upon the Narragansetts and to absolve the sachems; "We are very apt to believe that if matters came to a just inquiry concerning the cause of the war, that our Narragansett Sachems, which were subject to his Majesty, and by his aforesaid Commissioners taken into protection, and put under our government, and to us at all times manifested their submission...Neither was there any manifestation of war against us from them, but always to the contrary, till by the United Colonies they were forced to war, or such submission as it seems they could not submit to; thereby involving us into such hazzards, charge and losses..."{270 R.I. Col. Rec. Vol. 2 p.257} Thus was Connecticut confronted with exposure by another colony for the injustice of their part in the invasion if they continued their usurpations. Actually, smaller land disputes between Connecticut and Rhode Island continued on and off, perhaps the last of which was resolved after the year 2000.

However, contrast the words in the above letter with these written two months earlier from the trial court where it was said the Narragansetts there on trial did "trayterously, rebelliously, royetously and routously arm, weapon, and array themselves with Swords, Guns and Staves, etc., and have killed and bloodely murthered many of his said Majesty's good Subjects". When you plan to execute anyone, you need many justifying words especially when practicing injustice! Considering the statements, quoted earlier by Governor Coddington and Deputy Governor Easton just prior to the war, Rhode Island's government should have felt some discomfort in executing any of the Narragansetts. Those two men were Quakers, and there was considerable difference in the attitudes of Quakers and Puritans towards the natives. They were all Englishmen, however, and both were engaged in the same process of gaining control of land while facing the need to deal with the natives. They were well aware of the bloodshed (much of which was English blood) that a similar process had brought on in Ireland just decades earlier.

The Narragansetts had accepted some Wampanoags true, but it was, or could have been known, that that was a desertion from Philip. The Pocasset and Sekonnet Wampanoag had sought safety with the Narragansetts. Some English from the Puritan colonies fled to Acquidneck Island at about the same time. Ben Church took his family from present Tiverton to Duxbury early on and then to Acquidneck in March 1676, both moves for safety. {271 Church p.72}

Rhode Island felt it had to act like its neighbors and execute those Indian leaders and others who fell into their hands. Indeed Rhode Islanders did experience the wrath of the Indians after the invasion by the United Colonies, but they had failed to distinguish themselves from the invaders. Rhode Island did not execute all the Indians that fell into their hands, nor did they sell any as slaves out of the country, but they forced many into involuntary indentured servitude. Our national hero Roger Williams participated in the rounding up of Narragansetts for indenture.

Plymouth, as part of its war preparations had solicited, via a letter to Rhode Island, Rhode Island's assistance in the event of the conflict, anticipated with Philip, but Rhode Island's government avoided involvement until the Narragansetts turned on them after the United Colony's invasion of the Narragansetts.

Chapter Thirty-One

✦

How Far They Fell

History did not end in August of 1676, but King Philip's War did, and it was a watershed event in English New England's history and much more so to the native people of southern New England.

The Niantic/Narragansetts declined joining with the hostiles throughout the war and may have been prevailed upon to join with the English along with the Mohegans and Pequots in search and destroy missions in the last months of the war, but those may have been only "Western" Niantics. The survival of the "Eastern" Niantic village was allowed and appears to be the means by which the Narragansetts were eventually restructured. {272 Chapin p. 91} On March 28, 1709 Ninigret II was granted an area of about thirty square miles territory "to be used, occupied or managed by Indians only" {273 Boissevain p.53}. Ninigret the first died shortly before the war's end in 1676; his death may have allowed the "Eastern" Niantics to then assist the English.

The natives who remained in their native locales after the war sank into a new low state of existence; involuntary servitude in New England, coerced service in English war parties in the north, poverty, pauperism, alcoholism and probably mental depression. As previously noted, many went into life-long slavery in different climes. Many others fled west over the Hudson River where Governor Andros shielded them from the Puritans, others fled north, some of those joined the northern Indians and continued to battle the English.

From a point of many successes, the natives of southern New England fell to a terrible and complete defeat and never again would any aboriginal people come that close to reversing the European progress in the New World. Those natives considered as the hostiles paid a severe price for resisting and losing. Those who helped the English were better off for a while, but eventually they too lost the life they and generations of ancestors before them had lived.

Ben Church had succeeded in gaining the surrender and help of many desperate Wampanoags in July of 1676. For their reward of risking their own lives and limbs betraying their fellow Indians, they were assured their freedom and whatever bounty they could get from captured Indians. At a later point, some were allowed to farm some less desirable plots of land, allowed to farm, something Indian men never wanted to do, on land they could use but not own, a small fraction of the land their ancestors had lived on and used for perhaps centuries. They were solicited or coerced time and time again to serve in battle in the north against the French and Indians in the ensuing decades. "Libertie is granted vnto eight of the souldiers, Indians, which have been in the service, may sit down and plant at Saconett, Capt. Church accomodating them with land on condition that they shalbe reddy to march forth for the further psueing and surprising our Indian enimies; hee satisfying the Indians, shall have the whole prophettt [bounty] of such an adventure." That is one recorded example of what they could hope for. {274 Shurtleff p.225}

Uncas, who was about eighty-eight in 1676, had given the English his Mohegans as their first and continuous ally. They were said to able to maintain their traditional ways longer than any other surviving southern New England Indian society. Interestingly, why would the Mohegans, so faithful to the English, be the tribe that avoided English ways the longest? The answer would have to be that they did not want English ways and were allowed to keep their own, and this was due in part to the sincere appreciation of their help by some of the English such as Capt. John Mason and his decedents who blocked interference in the Mohegan world.

Chapter Thirty-Two

✦

Possible Lessons

While the rebelling Indians benefited in the conflict from the use of European guns, the English benefited from the aid of collaborating Indians. The natives failed to apply or learn from the example of the English, and failed to adopt a very important concept in waging war-you must unite all those who are confronted with the same problem as yourself and attempt to divide your enemies - exactly what the English did so well.

These events are long past and the past cannot be changed, but it can be reviewed and is subject to interpretation and reinterpretation. Pope Benedict XVI noted in 2005- "The past is not just the past. The past is always the past, it has something to tell us about what course to take or not to take."

If we conclude that what was done by the early English to the natives was basically wrong and we note that few of the English admitted any wrong, and that eventually they obtained all the land in New England (America?), does that indicate that not admitting wrong and indeed pretending justification might generate and sustain motivation towards goals and help achieve those goals?

If we believe and embrace the above conclusion, how does that affect what course we should take in our own personal decisions or how we want our society to behave?

This was not the first time that one society displaced another by one or another nefarious means, but not for long is it, if at all, glorified, as it has been for the American colonists.

It is probable that indigenous people found living in the New World in their various locations may have displaced earlier societies or groups dwelling at those locations. There are some indications of native displacements in stories written by colonists. For instance, it is written that Massasoit and another Wampanoag sachem claimed displacement by Narragansetts from some present Rhode Island land. The existence of two Niantic villages, the so-called "Eastern Niantics" and the "Western Niantics" with a substantial stretch of Pequot villages between the two Niantics on the coast of the Long Island Sound suggests that the Niantics may have been split apart at some earlier time . The Niantics who participated with Mohegans in assisting in English search and destroy parties may have been "Western Niantics".

These two examples are but displacements, perhaps by violence, but where life could go on, albeit less happily, but much as before. But what happened in many parts of the New World to native societies such as the Narragansett, Wampanoag, etc. was a virtual societal extermination by the Europeans.

The words "pretender", "pretense", "usurper" and "usurpation" were regularly used by English writers and clearly the concept of those words was understood. These words were used against others within and without the English world, but seldom was it fully recognized how pervasive the behavior identified by those words was in English conduct of those times.

Daniel Defoe (1660-1731) the author of ROBINSON CRUSOE lived during some of the years of England's colonizing. He was a prolific writer. "Especially noteworthy among his writings...was the satiric poem THE TRUE-BORN ENGLISHMAN (1701), an attack on beliefs of racial or national superiority, which was directed particularly toward those Englishmen who resented the new king William III because he was Dutch". {275 Ency. Vol.7 p.369} In his book, "JURE DIVINO" Defoe wrote a short poem in 1706 that applies to our subject viz. –

"The very lands [England] we all enjoyed
They ravished from the people they destroyed
All the long pretenses of decent
Are shams of right to prop up government
Tis all invasion, usurpation all...
Tis all by fraud and force that we possess
And length of time can make no crime the less." {276 Hill p.308}

Defoe was not just a prolific writer "having produced perhaps four hundred books and tracts", he also was a "brilliant...social thinker" {277 Ency. Vol.7 p.369} How much Defoe was thinking of the colonization then going on when he wrote the above poem we cannot know, but he, an Englishman, describes the process of colonization so well.

To take from others and leave them without and to go on in time with no mention of remorse, whether felt or unfelt, this was the observable behavior of the colonist.

There have been two main objectives aimed at in this work. One objective is to convince the reader of the immoral dispossessions of the native peoples, by the Europeans This probably applies to all or almost all the native Americans as victims of the Europeans. The second object aimed at is to bring to view the many instances of decencies and humanity, (notwithstanding some inhumanities) shown by many natives as noted by captives such as Mary Rowlandson, Mary Jamison and others captives as well as commentary by some European and American writers.

From Rowlandson's narrative I have structured five classifications of native behavior by my interpretation, and I have totaled each behavior.

Instances of charity	15
Instances of humane behavior	21
Instances of native reciprocity	6
Instances of native inhumane behavior	3
Instances of native cruelty	3

In addition, several times God's help gets the credit when it appears native allowances helped Mary.

Time and time again the hungry Rowlandson wanders amongst the wigwams of the temporary villages, stepping into wigwams and asking for food. Some refuse, but always some Indian gives her something, small portions indeed, but what was given to her must have come from very meager supply, obtained usually with difficulty.

Mary's description of what was obtained as food by the natives indicates both how versatile their gathering was and how little they usually had while on the move. - "They would pick up old bones, and cut them to pieces at the joints, and if they were full of worms and magots, they would scale them over the fire to make the vermine come out, and then boile them, and drink up the liquor, and then beat the ends of them in a Mortor, and so eat them. They would eat Horses guts, and ears, and all sorts of wild Birds...also Bear, Vennison, Beaver, Tortois, Frogs, Squirrels, Dogs, Skunks, Rattlesnakes; yea the very Bark of Trees...and provisions which they plundered from the English."

Mary credits God for the Indians' survival - "...strangely did the Lord provide for them; that I did not see (all the time I was among them) one Man, Woman or Child, die with hunger....I can but stand in admiration to see the wonderful power of God, in providing for such a vast number of our Enemies in the Wilderness, where there was nothing to be seen, but from hand to mouth." From those natives who struggled from day to day to scratch out something to eat, she was granted, from strangers, the charity of some small share of their lot. Individuals helped her who knew her not, who did not expect to gain from her captivity, or in any way, "own" her.

Not only did she frequently receive food from strange Indians, in addition she was surprised by gaining some feeling of safety while with them "...by night and day, alone and in company: sleeping all sorts together, and yet not one of them ever offered me the least abuse of unchasity to me, in word or action."

Several instances of reciprocation for favors received in the past can be picked out of recorded stories. It was written, perhaps a legend, that two sons of Huge Cole were taken captive in June 1675 by Indians at Swansea before the outbreak of hostilities. Brought to Philip at Mt. Hope, Philip sent them safely home as well as sending warning to Huge to flee Swansea. It was written that this was done because of some kindness received from Huge to Philip or his father Massasoit. {278 Hall p.103}

Hubbard noted this of the attack on Dartmouth: "Dartmouth... June 1676 [Mather says 1675 which seems correct] a Man and a Woman slain by Indians, another woman was wounded and taken, but because she had kept an Indian Child before, so much kindness was shewed her, as that she was sent back, after they had dressed her wound, the Indians guarded her till she came within sight of the English."{279 Hubbard p.41}

Hezekiah Willett was killed near his father's home in the area of Swansea know as Wannamoisett (now Bullock's Cove Barrington R.I.). In the diary of Judge Samuel Sewall it is written- "Saturday, July 11, 1676 Mr. Hezekiah Willet slain by Narragansetts, a little more than a gun-shot off from his house, his head taken off, body stript, Jethro his Niger, was then taken, [but] retaken by Capt. Bradford the Thursday following... [Jethro] Related that the Mont Hope Indians that knew Mr. Willet, were sorry for his death, mourned, kombed his head, and hung peag in his hair." It was indicated elsewhere that a party of Pokanoket (Mt. Hope) Indians came upon the body of Willet after he was slain.

I have presented in this work not only the decent behavior of the Indians, but some of the bad, all of which is derived from English sources, but it is the virtuous behavior that is truly impressive. Soldiers, warriors, men in combat times do too often commit unneeded acts of brutality and their society may be reluctant to punish them for such acts. But what cultures effectively compel, teach or encourage their members to share however little they have with those who have none? What cultures compel, teach or encourage their members to remember to return a kindness or a favor with no reservation for the color of the skin or difference of language? What cultures effectively compel, teach or imbue their men that they must not take advantage of the weaker sex to indulge their desires? The evidence is that these Indian cultures had considerable success in instilling those virtues.

The English seemed to have always felt justified in their activities wherever they settled. They might appease the natives or they might intimidate them, but they always expected to gain the land they needed, and they always needed more.

These Christians were able to use many religious quotes from their Judaeo-Christian traditions that might seem to support them in their struggles in the New World. They avoided, however, mentioning Christ's second commandment "to love thy neighbor as thyself" and his quite clear identification of who "thy neighbor" was in his parable of the good Samaritan.

When the war was going badly for the colonists, their preachers said that that was God's way to chastise them for their deviation from the correct path; and when the Indian effort collapsed, their preachers assured them that this was God's validation of his affection for his chosen people.

The Puritan interpretation of God's plan probably aided their usurpations, but they had other rationalizations that were also used and could have been used more if God had been used less or if not at all. They had achievements in the arts, in navigation, in science and indeed the law, the law (which they used so well that they could forget justice). They also had skills, inventions and the written word etc. all of which allowed them to feel superior and entitled to more than the "barbarians".

The natives, while not developing the same arts, riches, inventions, skills, or especially the written word, did live in societies that approached egalitarianism, which for those societies would seem a great asset, although not so viewed in much of rest of the world. Accumulation of any kind of riches was discouraged, and at least some tribes had annual public ceremonies in which those individuals that had accumulated excess goods of any kind could exalt themselves by giving away much of what they possessed.{280 Williams p. 197} No member of a village could starve while other members had available food. In those ways, their societies behaved better than most European societies. Indeed it could be said that England, at that period could be called a failed society. Pauperism and impoverishment were common, while others citizens lived with excess. Jails were full, even though punishments were severe. I suppose much the same could be said of much of Europe. Thomas Morton, one founder of the plantation at Wessaqusett just north of Plymouth, called Merrymount, and founded shortly after Plymouth, wrote: "If our beggers of England should with so much ease (as they) [Indians], furnish themselves with foode, at all seasons, there would not be so many starved in the streets, neither would there be so many gaoles [jails] be stuffed, or gallouses [gallows] furnished with poor wretches, as I have seene them" {281 Morton p.176}

The English government tried many times to rid the country of too many of the poor and the unlawful sort, and the colonies were seen and often used as a partial way of achieving that end. Why wouldn't this be considered a failed society? However, when we consider how many people in this world now speak English, we know that, in another way, it was a very successful society.

I am aware that some evolutionary biologists "claim that human moral intuition is an inherited, as opposed to a cultural acquisition." {Robin Blumner 5-7-07} In this theory, all humans have an inherent sense of fairness, decency and compassion that may arise in them regardless of what their culture or their religion may or may not have taught them. That probably is true, but surely what one is taught may either enhance or block such feelings. Any close study of history may reveal, in human behavior such enhancement or blockage. Why do we not find reports of English charity towards suffering natives during the war if all humans have a "moral intuition" that should have caused some compassionate acts? Two general answers come to mind: one, kindness towards an enemy is not apt to be reported or welcomed if reported (and its occurrence, if it happened, could be due to either an inherent sense or to a learned value); two, the teaching of an entirely negative evaluation of the natives could crush most compassion towards them.

Most of the English behavior towards the natives could not and would not have occurred without the learning of negative attitudes towards the natives. Not all Europeans accepted such negative learning. Two individuals quoted earlier, Gerrard Winstanley and the author of "Tyranipocrit Discovered" are prominent examples of Englishmen rejecting such learning. Some religious men, also quoted, held attitudes contrary to the general view i.e. Bathomule Las Casas and Rev. John Heckewelder.

It would be remiss to not note that the Puritan and Separatist colony records show that those governments were attentive to the needy within those colonies. They also reported helping the sick natives living near them during the times of the plague.

Unquestionably, a grave and irreparable wrong was done to the Indians. The survivors after 1676 must have lived with immense sorrow, loss of relatives and friends by death, servitude or removal into slavery, loss of favorite dwelling places and loss of access to resources needed and formerly used for subsistence. They also lost much of the ability to produce future generations of Indians.

Mary Rowlandson, after remaining in Mass. Bay colony with her reunited family, moved to Connecticut colony when her husband accepted a call to be the minister of the church in Wethersfield in April 1677. {282 Green p.25}

Mary's narrative was first published in 1682, We can't know if her husband who died Nov.24 1678 ever saw any draft of it. Her apparent admiration of her "master", Quanapin may not have been known to her husband. How many times in the remainder of Mary's life did her thoughts turn to times of her captivity and her contact with Quanapin?

The End

Glossary

Names of Indian locations or tribes not defined in text

Abenaki- natives of northern New England

Baquaug- river in north central Massachusetts now called Millers River

Cansatauga- this name appears to be Iroquoian perhaps a Hodosoonee village

Caughnawaga- name given to a splinter tribe of Roman Catholic Mohawks allied with the French

Cayuga- tribe of central New York state, part of the Hodosonee league

Cowesett- a Narragansett village, may have been located on Greenwich Bay R.I.

Kussoe – a tribe of the Carolinas

Manomet- Wampanoag village was located south of present Plymouth Massachusetts

Mashpee- Wampanoag village was located in present Falmouth Massachusetts

Mattachiest- Wampanoag village location not known perhaps north of present Plymouth

Montaup- (Mt. Hope) a rise of land in Bristol R.I., a Wampanoag village

Mystic- Pequot village located on river of the same present name in Mystic Conn.

Nipsachuck- location in Smithfield R.I.

Nashua- Indian name of the location of Lancaster Mass.

Natick- Massachusetts Indian village 25 miles south-west of Boston

Nauset- Wampanoag village area of east-most Cape Cod

Nemasket- Wampanoag village area near present Middleboro Massachusetts

Niantic- two villages in south-most R.I. and eastern Conn.

Nichewaug- Nipmuck village in present Petersham Massachusetts

Norwottuck- Connecticut River Indian village located near present Northampton Mass.

Patuxet- Wampanoag village at the site of present Plymouth Massachusetts

Pawtuxet- Narragansett village probably south of Providence R.I.

Penobscot- Abenaki tribe of southern Maine

Piscataqua- area about the river of the same present name that now divides N.H. and Maine

Pocasset- Wampanoag village found in present Fall River Mass. and Tiverton R.I.

Potowomut- Narragansett village near south shore of Greenwich Bay R.I.

Quabaug- Nipmuck village near present Brookfield Mass.

Rappahanock- area around river of the same present name in Virginia

Seekonk- name of an area now E. Prov. R.I.& Seekonk Mass. or a Wampanoag village

Sekonnet- Wampanoag village or name of area of the mainland opposite the east side of Aquidneck

Shawnees-Algonquin speaking tribe living in Ohio in the 18th century

Shawomet- 1. Narragansett village near present Warwick R.I., 2. neck of land now of Somerset Mass.,- 3. Indian village now Boston

Sioux- confederacy of tribes of a vast area from northern Wisconsin south through the Dakotas

Squabaug- Nipmuck village may be the same as Quabaug

Squaukheag- area presently in Northfield Mass.

Wabbaquassett- Indian village was near present Woodstock Conn.

Wenimesset- Nipmuck village on Warre River now New Braintree Mass. (also know as Menameset)

Sources

41 (anonymous) "a True Account...of Occurrences That Have Happened in the War..." 1676 excerpts from OLD INDIAN CRONICLES Drake S. ed.

30,37 (anonymous- "a factor") "Being a True & Last Account of the Present War ...Aug. 1676..." Excerpts from OLD INDIAN CHRONICLES Drake, S

Andrews, K. R., Canny & Hair editors- THE WESTERN ENTERPRIZE ENGISH ACTIVITIES IN IRELAND, THE ATLANTIC & AMERICA 1480-1650 pub. 1980

13 Arnold, Samuel G. HISTORY OF THE STATE OF RHODE ISLAND AND PROVIDENCE PLANTATIONS VOL. I Appleton pub. N.Y.1859

51,58,65,70,237,238
Baker, Alice C. TRUE STORIES OF NEW ENGLAND CAPTIVES CARRIED TO CANADA...1897

117-119, 243
Bartlett, John R. LETTERS OF ROGER WILLIAMS 1620-1682 Narragansett Club 1874

134,134b,135,137
Beer, George L. OLD COLONIAL SYSTEM Vol. I + II 1913 Macmillan Co. N.Y., N.Y.

104,105,108,112,113,120,124,125,128,132,162,232
Beer, George L. THE ORIGIN OF THE BRITISH COLONIAL

SYSTEM   1578-1660   1908 Macmillan Co. N.Y., N.Y.

48-50
Bicknell, Thomas W.   HISTORY OF RHODE ISLAND +
  PROVIDENCE PLANTATIONS VOL.1, 1900

273 Boissevain, Ethel THE NARRAGANSETT PEOPLE   Inter
  Tribal Series pub.   1975

110,111,121,128b,168,220
Bradford, William   OF PLYMOUTH PLANTATION   1856
  McGraw Hill   Modern Library   College Editions   Random
  House 1981

241 Brandon, William   INDIANS American Heritage Library
  Houghton Mifflin 1989

26,245 Burke, Charles T.   PURITANS AT BAY   Exposition Press
  386 Park Ave N.Y., N.Y.10016 1967

74,81 Calloway, Colin ed.   NORTH COUNTRY CAPTIVES
  University Press of New England   1992   Hanover, N.H.

126,264 Canon, J. & Griffiths, R.   OXFORD HISTORY OF
  BRITISH MONARCHY 1988   Oxford University Press N.Y.,
  N.Y. by permission of Oxford Univ. Press

100 Canny, N.   "The Problem of Social Control...English
  Settlements"   found in Andrews 1980

Cave, Alfred, A. THE PEQUOT WAR 1995 Calloway & Connell
  ed.

248,265,267,272
Chapin, Howard W. SACHEMS OF THE NARRAGANSETTS
  1931 Rhode Island Historical Society Roger Williams Press,
  E.A. Johnson Co.

10,33,175,176,206,250,251,253-257,259,262,263,271
Church, Thomas   THE ENTERTAINING HISTORY OF KING
PHILIP'S WAR 1st printing 1716 S. Drake ed. 1827   Simpson
edition 1999

169,171 Crosby, Alfred W. ECOLOGICAL IMPERIALISM 1986
Cambridge University Press

170 Diamond, Jared A POX UPON OUR GENES Natral History Magazine   Feb. 1990

2   Drake, James   KING PHILIP'S WAR A CIVIL WAR IN NEW
ENGLAND   Amherst University Press   1999

52,173,208,211,212,233,236,244,268,269
Drake, Samuel, G.   BOOK OF THE INDIANS   Antiquarian
Institute 1836

30,37,59,60
Drake, Samuel, G. ed. INDIAN CAPTIVITIES OR LIFE IN THE
WIGWAM   1851

41 Drake, Samuel, G. ed. OLD INDIAN CHRONICLES 1867

82,239 Drimmer, Frederick ed. CAPTURED BY THE INDIANS
1961 Dover Pub. Mineola, N.Y.,N.Y.

8,22 Easton, John, A. "A Relacion of the Indian Warre 1675..."
excerpts found in Lincoln 1930

38 Ellis, G. & Morris, J. KING PHILIP'S WAR H. Stiles ed.
Grafton Press N.Y.,N.Y. 1906

228 Emmet, Thomas A. IRELAND UNDER BRITISH RULE
Knickerbocker Press N.Y.,   N.Y. 1903

275,277 ENCYCLOPEDIA Funk+Wagnalls-Vol. 7 1973

224 Floyd, Candace HISTORY OF NEW ENGLAND Portland House Press 1990 N.Y.,N.Y.

85 Franklin, Benjamin "The Papers Of B. Franklin" L.W. Labaree ed. found in Washburn

219 Fuller, Oliver HISTORY OF WARWICK [RHODE ISLAND]

56,57 Gilbert, Benjamin THE CAPTIVITY OF BEN GILBERT & FAMILY written by William Walton 1st print 1784, excerpts found in Vaughan

14,15,172,202,203,235
Gookin, Daniel AN HISTORICAL ACCOUNT OF THE DOINGS & SUFFERINGS OF THE CHRISTIAN INDIANS... Dec. 1677 S. Drake ed.

95,153,166,199
Gookin, Daniel HISTORICAL COLLECTIONS OF THE INDIANS IN NEW ENGLAND 1674 Arno Press Wisconsin Historical Library 1972

1,3,4,282
Green, David L. "New Light on Mary Rowlandson" found in the periodical "Early American Literature" 1985

61,62 Gyles, John MEMOIRS OF ODD ADVENTURES... CAPTIVITY OF JOHN GYLES 1736 excerpts found in Vaughan

278 Hall, Jerome S. IN A PLACE CALLED SWANSEA 1987

122,141 Handler, Jerome S. "The Amerindian Slave Population of Barbados in The 17th And Early 18th Centuries" (article in "Caribbean Studies") 1969

75-79 Hanson, Elizabeth GOD'S MERCY SURMONTING MAN'S CRUELTY 1728 S. Keimer Philadelphia excerpts found in Vaughan

260b Harris, William "A Rhode Islander reports on King Philip's War...second letter of William Harris 1675" Records of the Rhode Island Historical Society

149,150 Heckewelder, John HISTORY, MANNERS, & CUSTOMS OF THE INDIAN NATIONS Historical Society of Pennsylvania pub. 1876

163 Higginson, Francis "New England's Plantation 1630" found in CHRONICLES OF THE FIRST PLANTERS Alexander Young ed. 1864

123,142-145,147,148,152,276
Hill, Christopher THE WORLD TURNED UPSIDE DOWN... Viking Press N.Y., N.Y. 1972

7,19,21,25,27,32,34,35,55,94,180-184,187-196,207,214,249,279
Hubbard, William NARRATIVE OF THE TROUBLES WITH THE INDIANS... BUT CHIEFLY 1675- 1676 pub.1677 S. Drake ed. 1868

258 Hutchinson, Richard "The Warr in New England Visibly Ended" 1677 (letter) excerpts from Lincoln 1913

87-89,127
Hutchinson, Thomas HISTORY OF MASSACHUSETTS BAY Vol. I (1628-91) Thomas Andrews, Boston 1795 L.S. Mayo ed. 1936

Passim Jamison, Mary A NARRATIVE OF THE LIFE OF MARY JAMISON dictated to James Seaver 1st pub.in 1780's ed. by J. Namias University of Oklahoma 1992

6,11,17,18,24,53,54,90,116,186,216
Jennings, Francis THE INVATION OF AMERICA... W.W. Norton & Co. N.Y.,N.Y. 1975

154,155 Jorgensen, Neil A GUIDE TO NEW ENGLAND'S LANDSCAPE Barre pub. 1971 Barre Ma.

165 Josselyn, John NEW ENGLAND RARITIES DISCOVERED Applewood Books

164 Josselyn, John TWO VOYAGES TO NEW ENGLAND Paul Linholdt ed. 1988

82 Kelly, Fanny NARRATIVE OF MY CAPTIVITY AMONG THE SIOUX INDIANS 1871 excerpts found in Drimmer 1985

115 Knowles, James MEMOIR OF ROGER WILLIAMS Lincoln, Edmands & Co. Boston 1834

240 Kolodny, Annette an article from the New York Times Magazine Jan. 3, 1993

129,130 Las Casas, Bartolome de IN DEFENCE OF THE INDIANS annotated by Stafford Poole Northern University Press

266 LaFantaise, Glen & Cambell, P SCATTERED TO THE WINDS OF HEAVEN… NARRAGANSETT INDIANS Rhode Island History Journal Aug. 1979 pp.67-83

LaFantaise, Glen THE CORRESPONDENCE OF ROGER WILLIAMS B.F. Swan ed. Brown University Press

131,133,136,138,139
Lauber, Almon W. INDIAN SLAVERY IN COLONIAL TIMES IN THE UNITED STATES 1913 Corner House Pub. Williamstown, Ma. 1970

140,174 LePore, Jill THE NAME OF WAR Knoph Press N.Y., N.Y. 1998

40,44 Lincoln, Charles- NARRATIVES OF THE INDIAN WARS
1675-1699 Scribner's 1913 New York N.Y.

177-179,218
Malone, Patrick M. THE SKULKING WAY OF WAR Madison
Books 1991

157,217 Man, Charles C.- "Native Intelligence..." Smithsonian Mag.
Dec. 2005

20,23,31,36,93,96,97,185,200,201,213,247,252,254,260,261
Mather, Increase BRIEF HISTORY OF THE WAR 1675-76
pub.1676 found in SO DREADFUL A JUDGEMENT
Slotkins & Folsom ed. Wesleyan University Press Middletown
Cn. 1978

63,64,66,71-73
Mather, Cotton MAGNALIA CHRISTI AMERICANA 1702
Excerpts from Vaughan

5,16 Mason, John A BRIEF HISTORY OF THE PEQUOT WAR
1736 Excerpts found in ORR ed.

281 Morton, Thomas NEW ENGLISH CANAAN first pub.1637,
1887 ed. Charles T. Adams

221,222 MOURT'S RELATION (two of the probable writers
Edward Winslow & William Bradford) Dwight Heath ed.
Applewood Books 1963

99 O'Brien, Marie & Conor Cruise A CONCISE HISTORY OF
IRELAND Beekman House 1972

Orr, Charles ed. HISTORY OF THE PEQUOT WAR 1897

146-148
Orwell, George & Reynolds, R. ed. BRITISH PAMPHLETEERS

Spottiswoode Ballantyne London 1948

46,47,80
Peckham, Howard CAPTURED BY INDIANS Trustees of Rutgers
University 1954

228b Puglisi, Michael J.   PURITANS BESIEGED Institute for
Massachusetts Studies 1991

98,102,106,107
Quinn, David B.   THE ELIZABETHANS AND THE IRISH
Cornell Press 1960

270 RHODE ISLAND COLONIAL RECORDS Vol 2

Passim Rowlandson, Mary NARRATIVE OF THE CAPTIVITY
OF MARY ROWLANDSON pub. by Samuel Green 1682
excerpts from Lincoln

156,158-161
Russel, Howard S.   INDIAN NEW ENGLAND BEFORE THE
MAYFLOWER University Press of New England 1980

197,198,225,242
Salisbury, Neal E.   "Conquest of the Savage 1620-1680" (dissertation)
1972   Univ. Of California Los Angelus. Ca.

39,42,43,234
Saltonstall, Nathaniel (N.S.?) "A New and Further Narrative of the
State of New England" (letter) 1676 excerpts from Lincoln

204 Schroeder, Betty Groff "The True Lineage of King Philip" New
England Historical & Genealogical register 144 July 1990

103 Shammas, Carol- "English Commercial Development and
American Colonization" excerpts from Andrews, K.R.

205,226,227,247b,274

Shurtleff, N.B.& Pulsifer, D. ed. RECORDS OF THE COLONY
OF NEW PLYMOUTH -LAWS- COURT RECORDS 1623-82
Vol. 5 1861

10b,97,246
Slotkins, Richard REGENERATION TROUGH VIOLENCE
Wesleyan University Press 1973 Middletown Conn.

101 Smith, Lacey B. THIS REALM OF ENGLAND 1399-1688
Heath Co. Lexington 1966, 1971

81 Steele, Zadoock THE INDIAN CAPTIVE- NARRATIVE OF
THE CAPTIVITY & SUFFERING OF ZADOOCK STEELE
1818 excerpt from Calloway

Snow, Dean R. THE IROQUOIS Blackwell Pub. Cambridge 1994

12 Thomas, Nathaniel (letter of ...Aug.10 1675) (to Gov.
Winslow?) found in S. Drake's edition of I. Mather's - BRIEF
HISTORY...

29 Underhill, John "News From America" 1638 excerpts from Orr
ed. 1897

28 Vincent, Philip, REV. "A True Relation the Battle English and the
Pequots" 1638 excerpts from Orr ed. pub.1897

56,57,61-64,66-69,71-73,75-79
Vaughan, Allen + Clark, Edward ed. PURITANS AMONG
THE INDIANS 1981 Belknap Press of Harvard University
Cambridge Ma.

83 Wakefield, Sarah F. SIX WEEKS IN THE SIOUX TEPEES 1st
pub.1863 Ye Galleon Press, Fairfield, Wash. 1985

85 Washburn, Wilcome THE INDIAN & THE WHITE MAN
Doubleday & Co. reprint of Yale University Press & New York
Public Library 1964

91,92,230,231
Webb, Steven THE END OF AMERICAN INDEPENDENCE
1985 Harvard University Press Cambridge Ma.

114 White, John, REV. "White's Brief Relation" cir. 1629
excerpts from CHRONICLES OF THE FRIST PLANTERS...
Alexander Young ed.

67-69 Williams, John THE REDEEMED CAPTIVE
RETURNING TO ZION 1707 excerpts from Vaughan

109,151,280
Williams, Roger "A Key to The Language..." 1643 J. Hammond
Trumbull ed. 1866

210 Winslow, Edward- "Good News from New England" London
1625 excerpts from CHRONICLES OF THE PILGRIM
FATHERS OF...PLYMOUTH... A. Young ed.

223 Wood, Bertrand NOMAN'S LAND ISLAND Mini News
Inc. Jewett City Conn. 1989

167 Wood, William NEW ENGLAND'S PROSPECT Alan
Vaughan ed. 1993 based on 1635 edition

114 Young, Alexander ed. CHRONICLES OF THE FIRST
PLANTERS OF MASSACHUSETTS BAY 1846 Charles Little
& James Brown Pub. Boston

210 Young, Alexander ed. CHRONICLES OF THE PILGRIM
FATHERS...1602-25 LONDON Little & Brown Pub. Boston
1844

About the Book

This work deals with observations on and interpretations of the English colonization of the area of present southern New England. This is a critical review of some of the contemporary English writings and quotes that deal with English interactions with the natives that lived there. The major event found in this work is King Philip's War of 1675-6 which resulted in the crushing of the natives in that portion of New England. This work includes much on the captivity of one English woman of that war, Mary Rowlandson. Her narrative (considered the most widely read captivity story ever written) and accounts and narratives of other English captives can reveal behavior in the natives that shows a humanity that is in great contrast to the savagery attributed to them by most contemporary writers. Mary Rowlandson's "master" is a Narragansett sachem whom Mary admires despite all the anti-Indian rhetoric she has been exposed to and adopted.

About the Author

Motivation to compose this work came originally from my reading a newspaper clipping kept by my aunt and presented to me when a teenager. The clipping entitled "The Story of the Indians Who Lived Here" was from the local newspaper. That story stirred empathy in me toward those Indians and, undoubtedly, a bias against those who dispossessed them. The desire to study and write about it came later.

I have completed college courses that apply to this subject in Western Civilization, psychology and sociology.

I have lived life-long within easy view of Montaup, the seasonal home of Philip's Pokanoket/Wampanoage, and within a few miles of the spot traditionally claimed to be where the body of Weetamoe, Rowlandson's "mistress", was found on the shore of the Titicut (Taunton R.).